IS A

• Early in 1973, Duncan Lunan startled the world by decoding Long Delayed Echoes received in the 1920's. He theorized these were messages sent by inhabitants of a planet of the double star, Epsilon Boötis, 200 light years from Earth.

• In October 1973, the Radio Institute at Gorki, U.S.S.R. reported receiving "radio signals from outer space in bursts lasting from two to ten minutes" and noted that "their character, their consistent pattern and their regular transmission leave us in no doubt that they are of artificial origin." Professor Kaplan of the Institute believes most of the signals come from civilizations somewhere in our galaxy—all older and more advanced than our own.

NOW! PUBLISHED FOR THE FIRST TIME
ARE THE LATEST FINDINGS OF
A. T. LAWTON,

world-renowned expert who set up a radio probe to evaluate Lunan's "messages" and other signals from outer space. The book discusses, in the light of known scientific data and reasoning, all the implications concerning man's first contact with alien civilizations.

Jack Stoneley, an ex-editor of a British Sunday newspaper, has, throughout his press career, contributed feature articles and covered news events on an infinite range of topics. He believes that the subject of this book is the most fascinating with which he has ever been involved.

Anthony T. Lawton, scientific editor of this book, is an authority on advanced electronics and has presented papers and lectures on interstellar communication and navigation in various countries.

He was a key member of a research team headed by Sir Barnes Wallis in the early 1950s working on swing-wing aircraft. Later he led one of the first British teams to shoot down target aircraft with remote-controlled missiles, and spent two years at Woomera Rocket Range in Australia.

Lawton has also designed electronic equipment for such aircraft as TSR2, Phantom and Harrier. He is an Associate Member of the Institute of Electrical Engineers; a Fellow of the Royal Astronomical Society, and a Fellow of the British Interplanetary Society.

Like the author, Jack Stoneley, Anthony T. Lawton is married and has two daughters.

IS ANYONE OUT THERE?

By JACK STONELEY
With A. T. LAWTON
Fellow, Royal Astronomical Society

WARNER
PAPERBACK
LIBRARY

A Warner Communications Company

WARNER PAPERBACK LIBRARY EDITION
First Printing: July, 1974

Warner Paperback Library is a division of Warner Books, Inc.,
75 Rockefeller Plaza, New York, N.Y. 10019.

W A Warner Communications Company

Printed in the United States of America

"Observe how system into system runs,
What other planets circle other suns,
What varied beings people every star."

—*Pope*

Have aliens been here before? Are they *still* here? Will man reach the stars? It is all part of an urgent field of research now being seriously investigated by the nations of the world, particularly America and Russia. For scientists are convinced, more than ever before, that man is far from alone in the restless universe.

CONTENTS

INTRODUCTION

On Tuesday, October 16, 1973, the normally impassive Russian daily newspaper *Tass* carried a remarkable report which read as follows:

"Academician Samuil Kaplan, director of the Radio Institute at Gorki, has announced the reception of signals of an unusual nature. The station is currently carrying out experiments on reception of signals generated by solar action in the upper ionosphere, but the signals mentioned by Dr. Kaplan do not appear to be of this type.

"The signals occur in trains of pulses after definite lapses of time and are repeated over a wide range of wavelengths from centimeters to tens of meters. *The possibility of these signals being of extraterrestrial origin cannot, at this stage, be completely ruled out.*"

A month later the American newspaper *National Enquirer* published even more emphatic statements from two top Soviet astrophysicists, Vsevolod Troitsky and Nikolai Kardashev, who first picked up these dramatic signals. Professor Troitsky, also of the institute at Gorki, is quoted: "They are definitely call-signs from an extraterrestrial civilization. This is only the beginning of some very exciting discoveries."

Dr. Kardashev said: "We have been receiving radio signals from outer space in bursts lasting from two to ten minutes. Their character, their consistent pattern and their regular transmissions leave us in no doubt that they are of artificial origin—that is, they are not natural signals, but have been transmitted by civilized beings with sophisticated transmission equipment. We can say the source is located in our own solar system."

Professor Kaplan believes that most of the signals are coming from one of ten civilizations somewhere in our galaxy—all older and more advanced than our own.

After these startling announcements from such normally unemotional sources, man must—more than at any other moment in his history—seriously consider the possibility of inhabited worlds other than his own. For signals such as these are *precisely* the type many scientists believe an extraterrestrial intelligence would use to attract our attention. So we *must* now ask: IS ANYONE OUT THERE?

At this very moment a communication satellite, launched by an alien race somewhere in space, could be orbiting Earth, attempting to make contact. In fact, its robot "brain"—a computer far in advance of any so far devised by humans—might conceivably be responsible for those signals received in Gorki, Russia.

They were not signals from Earth-launched satellites, said the Russians. And, they claimed, they could not be natural signals because they were reported regularly at set times several times a day.

More than 30 Soviet scientists are now seriously committed to searching for possible signals from aliens.

Troitsky conducts observations from four points in the Soviet Union—Gorki (Central Russia), Ussariisk (Far East) Murmansk (Far North) and Mount Karadag in the Crimea. Kardashev uses three points in the mountains—the Caucasus, the Pamirs and Kamchatka.

The signals—bursts of radio emission of two to ten minutes duration—were recorded simultaneously at two, and sometimes three, different points.

In England, Anthony Lawton, scientific editor of this book, is currently investigating radio operators' reports of strange long-delayed echoes, some dating back to the 1920s. Could any of these—like the Gorki signals—have been coming from such an Earth-orbiting probe, sent here by some other inhabited planet in our galaxy?

Early in 1973 Duncan Lunan, a twenty-seven-year-old astronomer from Troon, Scotland, caused a world-wide wave of speculation and controversy when he claimed to have decoded sequences of echoes from space —picked up in Holland in 1928 and '29—and, in fact, to have transformed them into actual charts or maps of known star constellations. He interpreted these as a deliberate method by some extraterrestrial intelligence to make us aware of their existence and to encourage a system of direct communication between their satellite and ourselves.

Lunan's startling theory is that the computerized probe, immaculately programmed to react intelligently to any response it might receive from Earth, was launched by inhabitants of a planet of the double star Epsilon Boötis, two hundred light-years away.

But, from his research so far, Anthony Lawton does not accept Lunan's reasoning in selecting Epsilon Boötis as the source of a possible probe. He says there are several explanations for those mysterious echoes received in 1928 and '29, which he is presently investigating. He is now certain that those echoes were produced in a way similar to that of others reported in recent years which can be attributed to natural disturbances in the ionosphere (the outer layers of Earth's atmosphere).

Lawton's current conclusions have been accepted

by other scientists who are acknowledged throughout the world as experts in the field of long-delayed echoes. Duncan Lunan's interpretation of the series recorded in 1928 and '29 has *not* been accepted. A more likely form of star map—possibly being transmitted by an alien probe—is shown, and explained, in Chapter 7. And those signals received at Gorki in the autumn of 1973 might, if correctly decoded, reveal such a map.

Lunan's star map of Boötes is composed from a specific sequence from the 1928–29 echoes. No other echoes known to have been picked up since can be arranged to produce the same map.

This book will fully present and analyze the claims of Duncan Lunan, and Anthony Lawton's alternative speculation, together with the views of other eminent scientists on those mysterious long-delayed echoes.

But it will also go much further by discussing, in the light of known scientific data and reasoning, all the far-reaching implications that man's first contact with another civilization would involve.

To present this fascinating possibility we shall, throughout this book, refer to the dilemma of an inhabited planet that could conceivably be attempting to contact Earth. It would have the most urgent reason to do so, as its highly developed civilization would have realized that its parent star, or sun, was dying. It would therefore have been forced to seek refuges within other star systems similar to ours; and artificial satellites beaming coded messages would be the obvious method of investigating other suitable worlds.

The planet we have selected to consider is assumed to belong to a parent star called Gamma Persei. This star really *does* exist. And scientists consider it to be of a type most likely to have been suitable for sustaining an intelligent life form—probably like our own. Gamma Persei is 113 light-years* from Earth. It is

*A light-year is the distance light travels in one year at the rate of 186,272 miles per second. This works out to six million miles.

thought quite likely to possess planets—though these cannot be seen by our telescopes. We shall assume that there are five planets, its two main ones being Perseus 1 and Perseus 2. We shall also assume that Perseus 1 has produced a civilization substantially more advanced than our own, whose members we shall call Perseans. (See Appendix 1, at the end of this book, for full technical details of Gamma Persei and its planets, and also where to look for the star.)

However, we do not present this book as science fiction. The grotesque situation of a planet such as Perseus 1 could be an appalling reality for some future generation on Earth. Our race too might be forced into that stark choice—interstellar travel with all its inherent and unknown risks, or, if we remain, slow but inevitable extinction due not to the death of our sun, though its death *is* an inescapable fact. But the hypothetical dilemma of the Perseans will be seriously and scientifically discussed in the light of problems now facing mankind in this restless century and in those to follow.

Overpopulation, pollution, famine, the drying up of our natural resources, and global suicide are all real swords of Damocles that may one day force us to abandon this green and pleasant land and, like the Perseans, seek new worlds in the inscrutable vastness of the universe. How would man face that ultimate challenge of survival?

Will the rate of his technological progress ensure his ability to reach for the stars? How soon will he conquer interstellar flight? Will he learn to harness the vast energy of the sun, reconstruct his own solar system, move across his galaxy at near the speed of light? And, perhaps the most critical question man must answer even before this century ends: Can the emotional development of the human mind get in step with the frantic rate at which new scientific horizons will doubtless be reached? If he learns to completely command the untold energy around him, will he also

13

learn how to avoid turning it upon himself in the anger or fear of a political dilemma?

If he finds a startling new interstellar "magic carpet" —some almighty type of spaceship propellant to carry him up and away to other worlds—will his own mind be sufficiently developed to qualify for membership in what might well be an already firmly established organization of super-races? Or will he still be motivated by that inherent "finger-on-the-trigger" impulse to shoot on sight anything that appears different?

The irrefutable proof that other intelligences are in the worlds about us could be the one thing that may unite nations for the first time in Earth's turbulent history. And can we now really doubt their existence?

Before man stepped out of his space capsule and made his historic walk on the dusty surface of the moon, talking openly about making contact with the inhabitants of other worlds would, to most of us, have automatically qualified a scientist for a special kind of laboratory—one with padded walls.

The subject of contacting other worlds made superb, hair-raising plots for science fiction, but few people really took the whole thing seriously. Today, as man looks deeper into the cosmos, the number of prominent physicists and biologists still refusing to accept the plausibility of life on other worlds is diminishing remarkably.

Scientists all over the world are now preoccupied with research into communication with extraterrestrial intelligence (now referred to in scientific journals as CETI). In October 1973 one thousand Soviet space scientists and engineers attended the International Astronautical Congress in Baku, Azerbaijan. Part of the event was a special meeting of the International Academy of Astronautics, dealing exclusively with the problem of contacting alien intelligences. Some of the world's leading radio astronomers discussed the results of their research, including Dr. Vsevolod Troitsky of the Radio Institute in Gorki, who has a team of researchers permanently engaged in attempts to seek out intelligent signals that may be coming from space. In addition, Anthony Lawton, who does not rule out the possibility of tracing alien signals, presented a paper outlining the space-echo investigations he is currently conducting in England.

The exciting news that man may soon launch his own orbiting satellites around alien stars was one of the highlights of the Russian conference. And some of that country's top scientists are convinced that we have the technological know-how to actually start this fascinating operation *now*.

The type of ion-drive rocket engines now in use with our unmanned satellites would enable probes to reach four of the nearest stars in flight times of four hundred to six hundred years—searching for alien signals as they traveled.

Although this is a vast time span on Earth, it is actually only a small fraction of the total existence of a civilized community. It means that for the first time in his history man can begin to reach for the stars. This speculation comes from conservative and cautious scientists at the Soviet Union's top academy.

It is one hell of a prospect. For if we can do this now, with a probe probably about the size of a Saturn rocket, consider what we will be able to achieve in the next few decades.

For the first time, a man-made probe has left our solar system. In 1973 *Pioneer 10* hurtled through the cosmic minefield of the perilous, meteorite-ridden asteroid belt between Earth and Jupiter. Twenty-one months after blasting off from Cape Kennedy, this 570-pound spacecraft survived the giant planet's fierce radiation—estimated to be a million times more intense than Earth's—and was flung off into outer space by Jupiter's mighty force of gravity.

Where its dreamlike journey will end, we shall never know. Millions of years from now it could still be groping farther and farther into the unknown. It will no longer be in touch with its Earthly makers, but who can tell what alien intelligence might then be plotting its interstellar wanderings?

In March 1974 a Mariner probe gave Man his first close-up shots of the pock-marked, moonlike surface of Mercury—that illusive world so near to the dazzling light of the Sun that even the finest telescopes could not unfold its secrets.

Our control of energy and power will increase phenomenally as our technology advances. Comparing presently available techniques for interstellar probes with those we *must* be capable of producing in the next hundred years would be like comparing the Wright Brothers' fragile little airborne craft to the mighty power of a Concorde. In fact, that historical flight by those original intrepid airmen could have actually taken place quite comfortably *inside* the empty shell of a jumbo 747 jet. Within the area of a superjet, the Wright Brothers could have taken off, flown, and landed—and there would still have been room left for the little bicycle workshop in which they built their brave little airplane!

At our present rate of technical progress, a space probe built within the next fifty years will probably take thirty years to travel to the nearest star. In, perhaps, a couple of centuries, the same journey should take no longer than seven years.

Ironically, it means that a probe built and launched now would be overtaken by those sent off many years in the future. The later ones could, in fact, report the safe arrival of the first one to leave Earth. However, later high-powered probes will probably be used to reach deeper and deeper into space.

The following dramatic conclusions are given in a paper presented to the Baku conference by Dr. Zakirov of the Institute of Applied Mathematics at the USSR Academy of Science. They are all endorsed by Professors M. Y. Marov and V. A. Egorov, also from the academy:

1. We already have the means to launch probes with ion-drive engines that will reach the nearest stars.

2. Gravitational disturbances from the sun, the galaxy, and the target star will not affect the major part of the flight, but must be allowed for during launching and parking in the orbit of a star or planet.

3. It is now possible to accurately program the thrust power during the journey.

4. Flight time would be about four hundred years to Barnard's Star (six light-years away) and six hundred years to stars approximately twelve light-years away.

5. The greatest navigational error expected is about ten percent, which could easily be detected and corrected.

6. A civilization more advanced than Earth's could migrate to its nearest stars by ion-engine propulsion in three to five percent of the lifetime of that civilization.

Late in 1971 the first Soviet-American conference was convened at the Byurakan Astrophysical Observatory in Soviet Armenia by the Academy of Sciences of the Soviet Union and the National Academy of Sciences of the United States. At that conference Professor Viktor Ambartsumyan, director of the observatory, said: "The discovery of the first extraterrestrial civilization could have colossal implications for man's destiny—it would be an event of the same order of magnitude as the harnessing of atomic energy, if not more important."

Among this distinguished gathering of world scientists were specialists in various fields, including astronomy, physics, radio physics, biology, computer technology, archaeology, chemistry, anthropology, sociology, and history. All agreed that present technology may be capable of establishing contact with extraterrestrial civilizations and that the cost of searching for them is, for all nations, justified. They also agreed that the discovery of alien races "can positively influence the whole future of man and greatly add to the total of human knowledge."

A joint Soviet–U.S. working group was established to coordinate all future investigation by both nations, who were urged to search for civilizations whose technological levels may be comparable to, or greatly in advance of, our own. The delegates also recommended searches, using the largest existing astronomical instruments, for "signals or evidence of astro-engineering in the radiation of a few hundred chosen nearby stars."

One such star could well be Gamma Persei, from where a desperate satellite probe for new worlds could have been attempting for centuries to contact Earth. And its fight to survive could be profoundly significant to the destiny of mankind. The traumatic record of the life and death of a single planet is also the life and death story of the universe. For at any moment in time, the end of a world is taking place. And perhaps, like our own world, it once throbbed with intelligent life.

If in fact an alien space messenger is at this moment orbiting Earth, what does it consist of and what is it attempting to do? Anthony Lawton shares the views of Professor Ronald N. Bracewell of Stanford University in California, one of the world's leading radio astronomers, who says that it is likely to contain a computer so advanced as to have some characteristics of a human brain, programmed and equipped to react as would an intelligent being.

Within the complexity of its mechanical mind would be stored vast amounts of knowledge of which we cannot yet be even remotely aware. In its electronic brain cells it would contain the history of the civilization which launched it. And it would automatically respond to any question we might put to it, once a mutual system of communication had been devised, and, in turn, ask questions of us.

One obvious reason why the probe would have to "think" and act on its own behalf is that reports back to its homebase planet could take hundreds of years, even traveling at the speed of radio signals—unless, of course, an advanced society had evolved a more rapid method as yet quite inconceivable to us. News of Earth now reaching a planet, say one hundred light-years away, would have to have been transmitted, by normal radio techniques, during the 1870s. That alien planet would now be getting a rundown on a horse-and-buggy age, when pioneer wagon trains were still rolling across the wild and woolly West.

Inside the finely tuned memory bank of an orbiting probe might be the full, dramatic commentary of the struggle for survival of a civilization such as Perseus —the whole desperate record of its dying sun and its plans for mass emigration into other star systems like our own.

Around the delicate metallic membrane of this robot intelligence would be the heavy armor needed to protect it from radiation attack and sniping meteorites as it maintained its lonely reconnaissance of our planet, waiting patiently for mankind to awaken to its pulsating cries from space, which may have been stifled by our centuries of unresponsiveness.

But how can it tell us of its presence so that we might unlock the interstellar Pandora's box for the untold secrets of the universe it might well contain? Its creators would have programmed the "brain" to begin full communication with us only when our technology was advanced sufficiently to make some kind of worthwhile allegiance. For what would be the point of such an allegiance with a backward race that had not even acquired the know-how to translate the first coded announcement of its presence?

How near are we to solving such a code? How could we distinguish signals sent to us by an alien probe from the continual stream that is being pounded

19

out by radio operators all over the world as they carry on their routine work of communication?

Quite simply. Whenever a radio operator sends out a normal communication signal—such as in messages between ships at sea—he gets back an echo as it rebounds from the ionosphere. And the time it takes to make a complete circuit of Earth and return to its source is precisely one-seventh of a second. If, on the other hand, a radio telescope aims signals at a distant object, such as the moon, the echoes would take longer. In fact, the farther away the target object, the longer the signal takes to bounce back. This is how radar telescopes tell us the distance to other planets in the solar system. But, of course, any set of signals directed at the same object must take the *same* time to return.

Now, if signals sent by a radio operator start to come back after varying lengths of time—say anything from one to thirty seconds—something quite extraordinary would have to be causing it. There have been many theories about what *might* cause such phenomena. And one, first put forward by Bracewell in 1960 and now being rigorously tested by Anthony Lawton, is that the computerized "brain" of an alien probe is receiving our signals and then deliberately retransmitting them back at varying times. In other words, sending them back to us in the form of a code—each delay being a significant part of it. When we are able to unravel that code, we may find that it contains an intelligible message.

So, the vital question is—*has* anyone yet heard long-delayed echoes (LDEs), and if they have, could they really be coming from an alien probe? It is a question that has been tantalizing scientists all over the world for nearly half a century. And we still do not know for certain.

However, to get somewhere near the answer we must go back to a chance meeting between Carl Störmer, a Norwegian professor, and Jörgen Hals, an engineer, in Oslo on a sunny day in the early spring of 1928.

Hals, who worked in the telegraph office of the Norwegian Postal Bureau, was a keen professional radio operator. He had been regularly tuning in to test signals from a new shortwave radio transmitter in Eindhoven, Holland—now called Radio Hilversum, but in those days known simply as PCJJ, which was its call-sign.

The tests were being conducted by a Professor Balthasar Van der Pol, director of Telecommunications Research for Philips of Eindhoven, the giant electronics group. Station PCJJ transmitted regularly throughout 1927, and Professor Van der Pol received reports from all over the world on the kind of reception gotten from the signals. Sometimes signals were broadcast in Morse code, usually the letters X, V, O, or S.

During that chance meeting between Störmer—a professor of mathematics at Oslo University—and engineer Hals, the latter claimed that when listening in to sessions of the PCJJ Morse signals, he had started to pick up echoes not only after the normal one-seventh of a second, but also after delays of three seconds. This just did not make sense, unless they were bouncing back from the moon.

At first Störmer did not believe it. However, knowing that Hals was a sincere man, a dedicated radio expert, and certainly no fool, he asked the engineer to write him a letter confirming what he had heard. The following is taken from the actual letter he wrote:

"I herewith have the honor to advise you that at the end of the summer, 1927, I repeatedly heard signals from the Dutch shortwave transmitter station PCJJ (Eindhoven). At the same time as I heard the telegraph signals, I also heard echoes. I heard the usual echo, which goes round the world in about one-seventh of a second, as well as a weaker echo about three seconds after the principal signal had gone. When the principal signal was especially strong, I assume that the amplitude for the last echo, three seconds after,

21

lay between one-tenth and one-twentieth of the strength of the principal signal. From where this echo comes, I cannot say for the present. I will only herewith confirm that I really heard this echo."

Professor Störmer then began his own experiments with PCJJ's Morse signals, which were being broadcast every five seconds. He had no success. By the summer of 1928 he was becoming pretty desperate, and decided to visit Professor Van der Pol to see if they could begin some joint experiments that might clear up the mystery. Störmer wrote at that time:

"On the twelfth and thirteenth of July [1928] I met Van der Pol, and we made some experiments at Eindhoven, but with negative results. Nevertheless, we decided to resume the experiments in the autumn, and we arranged that station PCJJ, instead of sending modulated signals, should transmit signals every twenty seconds, consisting of unmodulated waves in the form of three dashes closely following each other. No waves were to be sent between the various signals."

Nothing occurred to throw any further light on the puzzling situation until October 11, when a dramatic telegram from Störmer arrived at Van der Pol's home. That telegram sparked off the continuing controversy over the long-delayed echoes.

What happened was that engineer Hals had telephoned Störmer to say he was again receiving those three-second echoes on signals with wavelengths of 31.4 meters. Störmer had rushed over to Hals's home and soon after arriving there ten minutes later found, to his astonishment, that not only were the echoes delayed, but the times in which they came over the air actually varied from three to fifteen seconds! As soon as Van der Pol got Störmer's fascinating telegram, he began his own tests. And the following is his original version of what happened:

"I immediately arranged the same night a series of test signals to be sent consisting of three short dots in rapid succession, given every thirty seconds between twenty and twenty-one o'clock [eight and nine P.M.] local time. I listened with my assistant to the 120 signals. Thirteen echoes were observed by both of us. The varying times between the signals and the echoes being—8,11,15,8,13,3,8,8,8,12,15,13,8,8, seconds."*

In each case the signal transmitted and the echo that came back were of precisely the same radio frequency. This was proved because the signals and echoes had an identical pitch of tone. For a few signals Van der Pol slightly varied the radio oscillator after they had been sent. When the echo came back *its* pitch had varied too. Van der Pol continues:

"The echoes I heard were rather weak, and though their oscillation frequency could be easily identified to be of the same frequency as the direct signals, the three dots of the original signal could not be recognized in the echo, the latter being of a blurred nature, except in the one case where the echo came in three seconds after the signal, when the three dots of the original signal were very plainly audible in the echo as well."

Scientists at that time had their own versions about how this strange formation of delayed echoes was caused. Störmer thought they might be reflected from mirrorlike rings of particles millions of miles from Earth. Van der Pol thought they were caused by the wisps of electrically conducting matter in the upper ionosphere. Sir Edward Appleton at King's College, London, attributed them to radio waves scooting around the earth several times before being picked up. Appleton, in fact, did his own experiments using transmitters in England and Geneva—and he too heard distinct long-delayed echoes—delayed up to twenty-five seconds—during a radio transmission from Eindhoven in 1929.

We have now traced and interviewed the man who

*There are actually fourteen echoes shown here—not thirteen —an error that has been repeated ever since.

assisted Appleton in these experiments, and seen and photographed his actual handwritten notes taken in 1928.

Unfortunately, during World War II all research into the strange echo phenomena had to stop, but more experiments were conducted in England between 1947 and '49. At that time, however, man-made radio interference was much greater than it had been in the twenties, when Van der Pol was operating, and no positive results were obtained.

In 1955 Professor Bracewell, then in Australia, who was very familiar with the work of Störmer, Van der Pol, and others, concluded: "As the years go by without positive confirmation, the suspicion grows that the original observers may have observed signals which were not real echoes."

However, these delayed echoes obviously "bugged" him and in 1960 he suggested that they might have been caused by an alien probe trying to contact Earth. Writing in the scientific journal *Nature,* he put forward this dramatic idea:

"To notify the probe that we had heard it, we would repeat the signals back to it once again. It would then know it was in touch with us. After some tests to guard against accident, it would begin its message. *Should we be surprised if the beginning of its message was a television image of a star constellation?*"

Which brings us right back to 1973, when that remarkable announcement from Scottish astronomer Duncan Lunan was flashed across the world. He had, he claimed, deciphered those original echoes from the twenties, and he had evidence to show that they could, in fact, form the coded message from an alien probe, or satellite, in orbit around Earth. And from them he had —as Bracewell predicted—produced actual maps of star constellations.

On March 29, 1973, scientists crowded into Caxton Hall in London for a special meeting of the British Interplanetary Society, to listen to young Lunan defend his startling theory. The entire proceedings were filmed by the Columbia Broadcasting System for television presentation in the United States.

The following month, details of Lunan's "discovery" were published in the Interplanetary Society's respected journal *Spaceflight*. His theory is that the signals which had perplexed Störmer and Van der Pol in 1928 came from the double star system Epsilon Boötis —two hundred light-years away in the constellation of Boötes—the Herdsman.

Lunan composed a graph, using the echo delay times in conjunction with the sequence, or order, in which the original signals were transmitted (see Figure 1 in Chapter 6). As he first explained to me during an interview I did for the *National Enquirer* early in 1973: "To my astonishment, the resulting dots on the graph made up a map of an easily recognizable constellation of Boötes in the northern sky. The curious pattern of delayed echoes was actually a pattern of star positions."

At that time the *Enquirer* also quoted Professor Bracewell's immediate reactions in America: "The map of Boötes constructed by Lunan's analysis could be interpreted as a method of communication from another planet. If I wanted to tell you where I came from, and I couldn't speak your language, I could show you with a picture. Naturally, I am pleased to hear that the British Interplanetary Society is investigating these echoes. Their investigation could result in a shattering discovery.

"The space probe Lunan describes could never be seen from Earth, not even with the most powerful telescopes. We can't even see our own space vehicles circling the moon."

Anthony Lawton's immediate reactions were also enthusiastic: "Lunan's findings are staggering. The chances of different echo delays forming star maps purely by chance are ten thousand to one. If an alien probe does exist, we must interrogate it."

Lawton then made preparations to launch his powerful radio search for the probe which actually began later that year and still continues. He is also repeating the experiments carried out by Störmer and Van der Pol, but at wavelengths different from those originally used. He hopes to produce, measure, and study long-delayed echoes.

However, both Bracewell and Lawton are now having second thoughts on Lunan's findings. And, even from his early experiments and scientific research, Lawton has come up with alternative speculation which will be dealt with later in this book. For although his experiments appear to disprove Lunan's choice of an alien star that is trying to make itself known to us, and also the type of code it has used, he does *not* rule out the original Bracewell theory that a probe *is* orbiting Earth. And, if it is out there, it is more likely to be from a star system such as Perseus.

In Chapter 7 Lawton's reasons are given in detail and, for the first time, the mysterious echoes from the 1920s are explained.

ONE

THE ALIENS

Is anyone out there? Presently, the compilers of this book have no conclusive evidence that there *are* intelligent beings on worlds other than our own. Nor has anybody else.

But, conversely, neither is there proof—or even reasonable logic—for claiming that there are not. It is an irrefutable scientific fact that solar systems throughout the universe are being continuously created in precisely the same way as ours was. So is it not utterly irrational to suggest that wholesale duplication of systems of this kind should produce life on only one of them? Isn't it far more likely that *noninhabited* solar systems are the exception and not the rule?

Astronomical observation and analysis has shown that most stars are composed of elements similar to those of our own sun. Many of their planets, therefore, should have a chemical construction like Earth's. Some must be of comparable size and density, which means they could possess a similar atmosphere.

It has been proved that the same combination of the same natural elements, under the same environmental conditions, *must* produce the same end products. In other words, an extraterrestrial intelligence on a planet of our type which has reached our stage of development could, quite logically, bear a closer relationship to twentieth-century humans than did some of the strange, fumbling prototypes of ourselves that roamed Earth in prehistoric times. They are quite likely to possess the same sensory organs, and even to conform socially, to some degree.

These similarities, however, could only be feasible on planets of comparable mass, chemical makeup, and temperature, and only among inhabitants at the same stage of evolution. Any variance in these fundamental things would produce enormous divergence in every aspect of shape, size, social behavior, and in their systems of movement, reproduction, and communication.

It would, for example, be quite impossible for us to imagine the ultimate biological and intellectual perfection of an advanced creature who has occupied a world for a million years longer than man has inhabited Earth. Their scientific and social techniques would be as incomprehensible to us as a television set would have been to Neanderthal man.

Science fiction has produced just about every mind-boggling permutation of The Creature from outer space, and no one can really argue with any of them. For what could be more horrific than the tiny inhabitants of the creepy-crawly world if our own microscopes were to suddenly inflate to the fearsome proportions of dinosaurs? And there is no reason why —through some slight diversity in the way life first evolved on Earth millions of years ago—a form such as one of those, rather than that of a human, could not have been endowed with intelligence.

It is estimated that on our own small planet alone there are something like one million species of living organisms—each adapting itself to its own particular environment and its own special little niche in the intricate pattern of life. As author Walter Sullivan puts it in his book *We Are Not Alone:*

"If there is a way to live by swimming, fins will evolve. If there is a way to live by walking, legs will appear. If there is a way of life in the sky, some animals will develop wings. Mites have found a way to survive on peaks near the South Pole. Algae live in the scalding water of hot springs. In the perpetual night of the oceanic trenches, six miles below the waves or adrift in the high atmosphere, one finds life. The wonderful process of evolution has, over the billions of years, pushed life into every 'ecological niche' that one can imagine. As in the free-enterprise system, if there is an odd way to make a living, someone will discover it sooner or later and prosper."

Many of the familiar creatures in this exciting world about us possess remarkable senses to provide for their own particular needs. Birds have light, fragile frames—otherwise they could not get off the ground. Many fish can generate electric pulses, and snails' eyes are extremely sensitive to X rays. And man is like he is for perfectly logical reasons—his size and shape fit in ideally with the characteristics of his planet and for the kind of existence he has been destined to have on it.

It must, therefore, be accepted that extraterrestrial life will, by exactly the same rule, adapt itself to the peculiar characteristics of its own world. Those originating on the giant planets would quite likely be powerful, squat creatures with numerous stubby legs due to the great force of gravity on their bodies. On a very small planet one would expect to find tall, willowy, fragile creatures with storklike limbs.

Dr. P. M. Molton of the Laboratory of Chemical Evolution at the University of Maryland, in a paper published in 1973 in *Spaceflight*, the journal of the British Interplanetary Society, wrote:

"There are reasons why we have the shape we do, why we walk on two legs and have little hair. There are also reasons why fish are streamlined and bears have teeth. The reasons depend on what they do. Functional perfection for a way of life is a result of long adaptations, not chance, and the same process must occur on other planets."

NASA illustrated this by asking children to compete in designing a creature that would suit conditions on the moon. The result was a species that would need very thick and highly polished skin to prevent loss of valuable fluids and to reflect some of the sun's intense radiation, with multiple, translucent eyelids, like an astronaut's visor, to enable it to cope with both darkness and bright light.

The extreme heat and gaseous surface of a planet like Jupiter might produce a creature that would float beneath its own built-in balloon, feeding off organic compounds produced in electrical discharges in the upper atmosphere.

The intelligences we may one day encounter could have two legs or two hundred; they might be flat or round, they may walk, swim, fly, roll, slide, crawl, hop, or squirm. They may be hairy or bald, transparent or solid. They may have one eye, a thousand eyes or, though rather unlikely, no eyes at all. They may even be just shapeless masses suspended in an atmosphere.

What *is* certain is that they will take the form best suited to the planet on which they must exist and to the sun that gives them life. To argue that intelligent forms must be like us and evolve only in conditions like ours is downright Earthbound arrogance. For even Earth creatures are living quite contentedly in environmental extremes. The tough little larva of the West African midge, for example, has been known to enter a state of suspended animation by dehydrating itself for as long as seven years, after which, when placed in water, it swells, its heart starts to beat and, soon after, it is active and feeding.

In its suspended state it has survived for up to five minutes at temperatures of nearly four hundred degrees. If man can one day emulate the West African midge, his problem of surviving lengthy and distant explorations into space may be simplified.

All of which poses another intriguing question of evolution: Will man retain his present physical form as environmental demands alter over the centuries?

In 1973 a group of scientists gave some nightmarish predictions of how man might look ten thousand years from now, provided he survives that long. According to their startling prophesies—and from the results of computerizing some of the social changes already influencing humans—it seems we could all be something like inverted pear-shaped dwarfs with large heads, small bodies, and much shorter arms and legs. We could have no teeth, only one toe on each foot, and our bodies covered with soft hair like a monkey's!

A Dutch scientist is reported as saying we'll have to grow body hair to keep us warm as Earth grows progressively colder. The pear shape, he explains, will evolve from expansion of the human skull to contain a bigger brain capable of coping with our inflated intelligence level, while, at the same time, a fall-off in physical exercise will lead to smaller bodies and weaker limbs.

A dental specialist from Johannesburg forecasts the death of his own profession as our teeth disappear with the production of more and more soft foods. In fact, he claims, human teeth have been getting noticeably smaller for ages. Other research, based on studies of Egyptian mummies dating back to 1,500 B.C. and carried out by a team from the orthodontics department at the University of Michigan School of Dentistry, indicates similar trends. The reason is that man no longer uses his jaws and teeth for survival,

31

as he once did. In fact, half of the world's children have teeth that do not meet properly and therefore require correction.

And what about that one big toe? The Boston anthropologist who offers this theory says the smaller ones on our feet are pretty useless already and will become even more so. They came in handy when our ancestors swung from tree to tree, but shrank as we evolved.

One doctor from Sweden reckons we'll all grow feelers like thin twigs sticking out of our heads to prevent us from bumping into things. The reason? We spend so much time in the dark watching television! Perhaps that's going a bit too far.

But certainly if anything is going to happen to the delectable shape of woman in the foreseeable future, the international rag trade will want to know about it. In fact, one big British firm that manufactures brassieres organized a nationwide survey on "The Shape of the 1973 Woman" to discover what has been happening to those vital inches over the years. Thirty-six different measurements were taken from thousands of women and fed into a computer. The findings, which, in fact show that women are getting larger, will not only affect the fashion business but also things like the size of school desks and aircraft seats.

So, if in our own world of a million species even man himself is changing, the permutations of aliens' appearance must be infinite. Perhaps gazing into that grotesque world of the microscope will give us a far more likely view of them. Perhaps the bug-eyed monsters of science fiction are not so far off the mark after all.

For generations man has speculated on alien life forms. In the eighteenth century, Johann Elert Bode (creator of Bode's law, relating to a set pattern of distances between our planets) believed these planets to be inhabited by people who became lighter and more spiritual the farther they were from the sun. And his contemporary, Emanuel Swedenburgh, a Swedish scientist, wrote that during a series of dreams he claimed were "divine revelations," spirits from other worlds described themselves to him. Martians, the most elite of them all, were devout Christians. Of Venus's two races one was gentle and kind, the other was comprised of cruel and ruthless savages.

One of the most ingenious forms of an extraterrestrial intelligence is that envisaged by the prolific Sir Fred Hoyle in his science fiction novel *The Black Cloud*. This is a vast interstellar cloud or mist that absorbs its energy by surrounding a star. The cloud is made up of a variety of chemical compounds with a central "brain" region which can transmit and receive radio waves. The cloud is self-sustaining, can reproduce by seeding other suitable clouds, and is able to replace any section of itself as it wears out.

The habitation of another world might even be composed entirely of plant life. Some biological researchers claim that plants have been shown to actually register reactions to humans. In a television demonstration, one of a row of plants in the studio was mutilated. Electronic wave-detector equipment was placed near the plants and a number of different persons approached them individually. The equipment registered nothing until the man responsible for mutilating the plant drew near. Each time he did, the equipment registered a response.

Many people are firmly convinced that flowers and plants have physical and emotional feelings. Gardener Fred Streeter of Sussex, England—a radio broadcaster who was awarded the MBE in the Queen's honors list in 1973—actually talks to his flowers.

So does Jack Boyce, one of Britain's leading seedmen. On one occasion he sent out hundreds of leaflets to people in his village in Cambridgeshire, telling them how plants respond to love and care. He is reported to tell his tulips things like, "You are beautiful this morning. You are giving me a great deal of pleasure."

He claims it has the same effect as when two teenage lovers hold hands in the moonlight—"It brings them forth into their full blossom."

"Plants are like humans," he insists, "they are living things. A great deal of serious scientific work has been done in America. In one test a group of plants were ruthlessly destroyed and shortly afterward another group nearby wilted from fear and fright."

Certainly plant life might be flourishing profusely on other worlds. At the Manned Spacecraft Center in Houston, scientists have found that vegetables planted in soil brought back from the moon by the Apollo astronauts grew as well as those planted in various types of Earth soil. There should, therefore, be no problems of setting up lunar greenhouses if man sends a colony to the moon.

However, we shall assume that intelligences with which contact may be made would be in some tangible form that we could comprehend. We shall assume they would be equipped to sense light and sound, though there may be many alien species that do not require eyes or ears for this purpose. They may have developed alternative sensory techniques, such as a natural, built-in sonar system like some Earth creatures possess. Eels, for instance, can emit electricity to stun their prey. Some aliens may be highly sensitive to magnetic or radio sources.

One wonders how much influence a creature as intelligent as a dolphin might have had on the world if it had developed arms and legs along with its quite versatile and extraordinary brain. Intensive research has been going on for years in America and elsewhere to understand more about the dolphin's wonderful world of sound, with its echo-detection system that enables it to locate objects and to distinguish shape and size.

Many fascinating studies are taking place to discover how these friendly creatures are able to pass on information between themselves and appear to virtually read one another's minds. There are many reports of dolphins helping sick or injured colleagues, standing in as "midwives" to help with births, fostering and adopting baby dolphins, and even helping to rescue humans in distress. Men following the pioneer work of neurologist Dr. John Lilly in Miami, Florida, hope to eventually perfect a method of talking to the dolphins.

But whatever form of intelligence an alien might possess, the range of its physical shape and size would be vast. Certainly the gravitational force of a planet would be an influence. To the squat inhabitants of a massive planet with a powerful gravity field, man might appear as a weak, spindly creature. To those of a tiny world, he might resemble a small, powerful dwarf. There may be worlds to whose inhabitants we would seem as insignificant as an ant, and others where man would be a Gulliver, able to crush a city full of proud little people.

Many Americans can still recall the blind panic that followed a fictitious radio news bulletin announcing that Martians had invaded Earth. Actor Orson Welles was introducing an adaptation of H. G. Wells's novel *War of the Worlds*, but listeners who missed his opening remarks were petrified to hear news flashes of grotesque, insectlike giants and death-ray guns complete with weird sound effects. Taking these news flashes for real, people stampeded half-dressed into the streets and stumbled in utter confusion across open fields. Cars careened crazily in all directions through the streets of crowded towns and cities.

Could this hysterical episode back in 1938 be an indication of how Americans would react if an alien race *did* actually make contact? Would the shotguns be blasting at everything in sight? Would mass, uncontrollable panic overrule logic before our extraterrestrial visitors had a chance to make known their intentions?

In the late fifties a research group set up by NASA

interviewed a large number of specialists to study the long-term effects of space exploration. Part of the report, which was later submitted to the federal government, did not rule out public hysteria even if contact with aliens was made merely by radio.

It was therefore recommended that studies continue to attempt to find out how people would be emotionally affected by such contact, and also how previous societies throughout history had reacted when faced with dramatically unfamiliar events. The report raised the question: How should the public be told of an extraterrestrial encounter if one occurred—or, in fact, should they be told at all? So much bug-eyed monster material has been absorbed through science fiction novels, films, and television serials during the last few years that it is likely the average citizen would automatically assume anything from out of this world was here for only one reason—to exterminate us and take over our planet. Mob-rule philosophy might well be "Let's get them before they get us!" The results of such a showdown are pretty obvious.

Aggression could be the farthest thing from an alien's mind. The fact that his society had advanced sufficiently to achieve interstellar travel would indicate that it must also have learned to live without war, otherwise it could not have survived long enough to reach such an exalted technology. And unless a take-over of Earth was essential to its very survival, its interest in us would most likely be purely academic—just as we might scrutinize some lower life form by turning over a few sods of garden soil.

Our space callers might even be philanthropists, only desiring to help sort out our global problems with sober advice based on their own solutions to similar crises in their distant past. Whatever social and scientific knowledge they felt disposed to impart would certainly be of infinite benefit to all mankind.

So wouldn't it be more sensible to listen to them before trying the John Wayne up-and-at-'em approach of a TV western? Provided we all kept our cool, there is no reason to believe that a superior society, one which would know we were noncontenders for the intelligence-and-technological stakes, would wish to destroy what would obviously be most interesting specimens to study.

But, of course, how can we know? We can only hope that we won't meet those Wellsian death-ray gangsters and that the aliens we eventually detect will not belong to the power-crazed variety described in a letter to *Scientific American* by physicist Freeman Dyson of the Institute for Advanced Study at Princeton: ". . . An intelligence that may be a cancer of purposeless technological exploitation, sweeping across a galaxy . . . a technology run wild." Logically, this would seem unlikely. Frantic power seeking and aimless aggression are normally associated with fear, inadequacy, and instability. Once a society reaches the mental nobility of a super-race, it no longer needs to prove itself by pointless intimidation.

When the day comes—which may not be far off—when contact with an extraterrestrial intelligence superior to our own becomes a stark reality one can only hope and pray that our world leaders will, for once, refrain from any kind of arrogant one-upmanship or face-saving show of strength.

In a Wellsian confrontation our most powerful weapons would still be regarded as primitive and obsolete compared to the techniques of a race even a hundred years ahead of ours. This would be one influx of immigrants whom we would be foolish to regard as second-class citizens. They would wield the bargaining power; *they* who would hold all the top cards in a fearsome poker game in which the jackpot could be our total extermination if we attempted to call their bluff.

Let us hope that some military early-warning system does not misinterpret a simple message of goodwill and cooperation from some interstellar advance party.

A fatal misunderstanding of intent could so easily be made by either side; how would an alien distinguish between friendship and intimidation, between love and hate, or, for that matter, between right and wrong? Why should their moral and social values be even remotely in accordance with our own? After all, we adapted ours to a pattern best suited to the particular lifestyle we chose to pursue.

It would have taken only some small modification in our early evolution to have produced quite a different set of laws and codes. Justice and humanity in the mind of a man might well constitute downright intolerance and aggression in the philosophy of an alien. Knowing this, it would surely be prudent to accept any form of approach by extraterrestrials—short of death-ray guns—with a completely open mind until, we would dearly trust, a friendly understanding was assured.

What type of intelligence would be likely to find it worth their while to contact us?

Of course, to arrogant and egotistical man, the answer would be any aliens who were able to signal Earth. Carl Sagan at the Center for Radiophysics and Space Research at Cornell University, New York, in a paper published in the autumn of 1972, does not share that conceit. He suggests that extraterrestrials substantially ahead of us will have developed technologies and discovered laws of nature that are quite beyond our comprehension. In fact, they would appear to us as "sheer magic."

There might exist a communication "horizon" between distinct groups of civilizations. Any of them further advanced than us by more than a thousand years might not even be interested in contacting Earth, suggests Sagan. They'll be too busily engaged in interstellar information swapping with their mental equals. To them, we may be like the inhabitants of New

38

Guinea, still using runners or drums to carry messages between tribes, quite ignorant of the vast and sophisticated international radio and cable traffic passing over, around, and through them.

Would such societies be concerned with us any more than we are concerned with our bacterial forebears? We may study microorganisms, says Sagan, but we do not usually communicate with them.

So, if you woke up this morning feeling like something that crawled out from under a stone, remember that to some advanced civilizations, you could be just that!

This reasoning also puts into proper context one of the favorite theories of some flying-saucer enthusiasts —that those heaven-sent crafts are launched by superior beings who only wish to show us the way to a better life. This very noble idealism would appear to be somewhat wishful thinking by those who are rather too eager to take a rose-colored view of a candy-floss universe full of Supermen and boy Robins overflowing with good deeds for all mankind. They may be perfectly at home on the cereal boxes of our TV screens, but it is most unlikely they'll be any part of the harsh, practical philosophy of a greatly advanced intelligence.

For any reasonable kind of tête-à-tête between man and aliens it would be essential that the gap between them—either culturally, technologically, or biologically—is not too wide. If future interstellar travelers from Earth encountered, for instance, an alien world which was on the evolutionary level of one of our ancient ancestors, such as Cro-Magnon man (who existed thirty-five thousand to fifty thousand years ago), what chance would there be of any exchange of knowledge? And if that alien happened to be like Australopitheous man, who roamed our forests half a million years ago, trying to communicate would be just about as futile as attempting to pass the time of day with a dinosaur.

39

Differences of a million years—or even three hundred million years—between alien technologies are highly probable. So, if the intelligence we contacted was one of those on the top rung of the evolutionary ladder, we could virtually guarantee that no useful communication could take place.

We might just be able to grasp cultures five hundred or possibly a thousand years ahead of our own. But the tools, vehicles, and techniques of a race ten thousand to a hundred thousand years ahead would be completely beyond us.

Whatever form or level of intelligence our first alien visitors may possess, there will probably be many preliminaries before any physical contact takes place. There must be the detection of their radio signals over distances of many light-years; the tracing of unmanned space probes in our solar system; the locating, perhaps, of laser beams or stars containing artificially induced flares intended as beacons, and the establishment of a mutually understandable code.

All these will be discussed later in this book. And to illustrate them more dramatically we shall associate them with the kind of urgent, underlying reason an extraterrestrial intelligence might have for wishing to investigate Earth. Interlinked throughout this factual documentary of the universe will be a "progress report" of one alien world that could be just like so many others. It is a planet whose star we *know* exists and which could well be trying to contact us. . . .

TWO

OPERATION SURVIVAL

"Top secret—your eyes only!

"Our sun is dying. Of this there is no doubt. Our astrophysicists and astronomers are in global agreement. A committee of heads of state and world scientists is being convened to draw up plans for the most vital project in the history of our race—Operation Survival.

"It is known from extensive surveys that no other planet in our solar system can be made permanently habitable. It is also apparent, from recent expeditions to our companion star, that it, too, has no planets capable of supporting life. If we are to survive, we must go elsewhere. The period remaining before evacuation must begin, the percentage of our race that can be transported, and the eventual system of selection, are being calculated by our main computer complex.

"It is imperative that this document be regarded as strictly confidential and should be destroyed, as soon

41

as its contents have been read and understood, so that public control can be maintained at this critical time."

About a thousand years ago—perhaps in 974 A.D.—a confidential document such as this might well have been circulated to key government officials and top scientists on one of the many planets in our galaxy now believed to be inhabited by intelligences far in advance of our own. For the purpose of this book, we shall assume that planet was Perseus 1.

Its sun, belonging to the binary star system Gamma Persei*—113 light-years from Earth—could, at about that time, have been near to entering the first stage of its celestial death—involving a fearsome, savage eruption which would inevitably bloat it into a growing inferno of unimaginable fury, cremating anything in its path.

The inhabitants of the planet Perseus 1—a race we shall estimate as being, at that time, some three hundred years more scientifically advanced than we are now, and whom we shall refer to as the *Perseans*—would have known their world was to be destroyed. Today, centuries later, a probe such as some scientists believe is orbiting Earth attempting to contact us, could well have been launched by a civilization like that of the Perseans.

Their star is of a type astronomers believe could support intelligent life as we know it. And by now—if that race had found a way to survive cremation from their own sun as it burned itself out in one last enormous breath of fire—their technology would be some thirteen hundred years ahead of man's. Sending satellites to other solar systems like ours to search for new, habitable worlds would be well within their scientific range.

One has only to consider the progressive stages of man. For about four hundred thousand years his life-

*See appendix 1

style remained virtually unchanged. He used the same primitive tools and his methods of survival were little different from those of the other creatures around him.

Yet in the last couple of centuries alone he has progressed from the steam engine to the nuclear bomb, from cotton mills to computers, from hot-air balloons to manned satellites around Earth, spaceships to the moon, and the first space probes to leave the sun and drift out to the stars. With each recent decade his technological evolution has accelerated at such an explosive rate that even the most conservative observers accept that the next hundred years—a mere moment in the galactic time scale—must produce social and scientific innovations beyond our wildest dreams—or, perhaps, nightmares.

Imagine, then, the stage of development the human being will have reached a thousand years from now.

The Perseans would have progressed through precisely the same kind of biological evolution that first produced a life form with all the intelligence, emotion, and frailties of a human being. And, as we are estimating that their species would have had longer to develop, we must assume that they discovered how to move, communicate, love, and annihilate each other many centuries before we did. They would have been sending astronauts into space hundreds of years before the Normans invaded Britain, and almost a thousand years before Christopher Columbus sailed to America.

While armies on Earth were still hurling rocks at one another, the technologically sophisticated, but still socially maladjusted, Perseans would have been blasting guided missiles across their violent world. At about the time Imperial Rome was falling under the onslaught of barbaric tribes, the Perseans would have been blasting each other to kingdom come in their final and most horrifying nuclear confrontation.

But from the terrible resulting fallout of material and moral devastation there would have emerged a clean, new society eternally immunized against it ever

43

happening again. From the radioactive ashes of that hysterical period in its history would have blossomed a far more mature and balanced race, dedicated to reestablish a global togetherness that would never again be divided by barriers of wealth, politics, religion, or race.

It would have taken almost a century to awaken from that long and agonizing nightmare, and to finally wash away the grim afterbirth of the nuclear monster their ancestors had created. Only the fittest of those who had evaded instant annihilation would have been able to cling on to life.

But with the new dawn that must have eventually filtered through that long, black night of death and devastation would have been bred a special kind of courage, and the will to create a better society, which could only arise from a catastrophe such as this. It would also have awakened a long-dormant ingenuity and resolve among the survivors—a new and vibrant kind that had been so sadly lacking in the nonchalance and aimless complacency that had started to pervade all its nations.

Survival would mean ingenuity and cooperation on a scale which they could never before have achieved. A stringent global economy, a rigid system of law and order, an inflexible moral code—all of these things would have become established as the only way to preserve and expand the few uncontaminated natural resources of their sick and ravaged planet. Those who deviated from the accepted code of survival in this brave new world would have been ruthlessly removed until, as each generation filtered itself of the socially corrupting remnants of its ancestors, there finally evolved intelligence far greater than ever before.

Fortunately, most of the stored-up knowledge of the Perseans' scientific and cultural institutions would have been salvaged from the carnage of their nuclear insanity. Now, their resources replenished, they would be progressing more rapidly than ever before, and at a much better-planned technological rate.

Social advancement too would have kept pace. With poverty, disease, and overpopulation totally controlled, biologists, physicians, and surgeons would have more than doubled the normal life expectancy of its race, and at the same time prolonged mental efficiency so that the most astute brains of the species could continue to absorb and conceive vaster amounts of knowledge for the benefit of all.

Would man, too, be able to drag himself up from the aftermath of such an all-out nuclear encounter? History is blemished by the rise and fall of civilizations, though none of such awesome magnitude as that now threatening our own. Let us hope we shall never have to know.

And one wonders how long the bomb can remain just an inactive deterrent . . . the forbidden fruit in some global Garden of Eden. You can't slap a patent on it. Smaller nations must soon add its catastrophic power to their armories. Some of them will be emotionally unstable societies, easily roused to national frenzy over their own precious cause—often one whose flimsy logic will be lost in ancient history.

Would a fanatical revolutionary who could drive home his message with a nuclear sledgehammer even stop to consider the inevitable consequences to the rest of the world? Would either side have kept its itchy little finger off the button to eternity in the last Middle East skirmish?

Some historians and sociologists believe that if mankind can refrain from using nuclear weapons for a hundred years longer, he should by then have accepted an interracial unity that will have successfully and permanently outlawed war. And it is virtually certain that by then he will have the medical and scientific knowledge to ward off any other threat of extinction from natural hazards.

Fortunately for us, our sun is not likely to suffer

the rate of Gamma Persei for a very long time. How would we know when that celestial doomsday was approaching? How would the Perseans have known?

The first ominous clue might have been found during routine scientific checks on the stream of infinitesimal particles, called *neutrinos,* that can only emanate in quantity from a sun. Researchers would have noted a slight increase in the rate at which these neutrinos were arriving at their planet. Little real significance may at first have been attached to the abnormally high readings, probably considered by most scientists to be merely some temporary phenomenon that would correct itself.

But as the levels began to increase alarmingly, more searching tests would be taken and computerized. One by one they would rule out each possible alternative to the one interpretation they feared. There would then be no doubt whatsoever that their sun's central core was approaching a critical stage and was, in fact, in its first phase of dying. One vital question would remain: Exactly how much time had they left before their beloved planet became consumed in the incinerating embrace of its death throes?

This fearful process of annihilation is not wild science fiction fantasy. At every moment, violent interstellar convulsions exactly like this are happening to some dying star somewhere in the universe. And nothing can prevent these convulsions from one day overtaking our own sun, once it finally burns up the hydrogen in its core.

When this does happen the sun will first begin to collapse into itself like a soap bubble being sucked back into a pipe. But before this condition progresses very far, the stored-up helium at the center, into which the hydrogen has been converted over the many millions of years of its life, undergoes various reactions—producing other elements such as neon, carbon, and oxygen. Meanwhile the outer layers of the sun will expand into a massive red giant, 250 times its present diameter. It will then continue to expand until it completely engulfs its closer planets, including Earth. The seas will dry, the rocks will glow, the earth will shrivel and crack, and all life will cease to exist for eternity.

Exactly when this catastrophe will occur, no one can tell—probably not for another five thousand million years. But it will. However, there will be enough time, once the first evidence occurs, for man to plan his method of escape to some other worlds—just as Perseus 1 could have been doing a thousand years ago. There will be plenty of warning signs. Our sun is not the type of star that shatters itself into a nova explosion in only a few suicidal seconds, as some of them do, destroying its system of planets in one furious outburst that can happen at any time, without warning.

The unfortunate planets of a star likely to end its heavenly days in this insane way would have no chance of moving out of the way. A sudden, abnormally massive buildup of energy beneath the star's surface, following an initial collapse, would rapidly bellow it out to grotesque proportions, blasting it into space—collapsing and inflating at a speed that even our national economy could never copy, even in the erratic 1970s.

Our sun will have a more lingering death. After gradually expanding into a planet-blistering *red giant,* it will begin to collapse, until, after a few hundred million years, it will calm down into the lonely insignificance of what is termed a *white dwarf* star—a tiny, phantom world of useless matter, a little larger than Earth.

As their atom particles collapse into a tight mass, some stars—originally many times larger than our sun —shrivel to only a few miles in diameter. This means that they become so dense that a teaspoonful of it would weigh thousands of millions of tons. If it were possible to drop a fistful of this mass on Earth, it would simply go right through to the center, making our world a few billion tons heavier.

47

Suns at this stage are termed *neutron stars*. Until a few years ago, varying radio signals being emitted from some of these dense little bodies—called *pulsars*—were thought to be messages to Earth from an alien planet. Now it is believed the pulsar's rotation caused the variations.

The number of known pulsars is now more than one hundred. Some of their pulses have the rapid, high-pitched cheep of a squawking youngster—others the slow, rusty croak of old age. The junior of them all is in the Crab Nebula, whose colossal outburst of light was recorded by Chinese astronomers in 1054 A.D. Today, we can see that outburst as a giant, ragged, luminous cloud lit up by the energy of a tiny flashing "lighthouse"—the leftover pulsar of a star ten times heavier and a million times brighter than our sun.

Even a pulsar may not be the final stage of a dying sun. Some scientists now believe that a far more fantastic thing can happen to a really massive star—one, perhaps, fifty times bigger than our sun. It can, they say, become a mind-boggling *black hole*.

If one of these monsters collapses in on itself, its immense gravitational pull would be so ferocious that nothing could withstand it. Its size would shrink to a point of no return—and yet its phenomenal gravity would remain, dominating every other force.

The normally accepted physical laws of space would no longer apply to such a transformation. To start with, it would completely reverse the original conception of the universe as a vast explosion splaying matter deep into space. A black hole would produce a massive "implosion"—sucking everything inwards toward its center because of the unimaginable force of gravity emanating from its tiny, but frighteningly dense, nucleus.

Anything that came within its range—even other stars—could be sucked in. A spacecraft would be engulfed from vast distances. And once inside it could never escape. Nothing could. Not even light.

Because of this, it is impossible to "see" a black hole. Even though it may be white-hot, its dazzling light would be dragged back again before it could get away from the fearsome suction of its gravity. In other words, the escape velocity of the surface of this concentrated body—only a few miles in diameter—would be greater than the speed of light. Therefore a particle of light, or *photon*, would fall back to the surface before it could be observed from great distances.

So, if a black hole can emit no light, how does anyone know it's there, for one was claimed to have been identified in May 1973. It is in the constellation of Cygnus—the Swan. Astronomers can spectroscopically identify a vast supergiant star which moves alternately nearer to and farther from Earth every few days. This, they say, indicates that the star is rotating around something which cannot be seen but must have a massive pull of gravity to alter the position of its colossal companion.

It was also noticed that the giant star became brighter or dimmer as it rotated—an effect thought to be caused by the black hole drawing gas from it. Further proof was added when scientists from University College in London, using instruments contained in a space satellite, found that X rays from the invisible monstrosity varied in intensity according to the to-and-fro movements of the visible star. And these X rays must have been emanating from the gas sucked in by the black hole.

The area of a black hole from which emitted light or radio signals cannot escape, is called the *absolute event horizon*. An original star that caused this incredible force field would have collapsed deep inside the event horizon—in fact, virtually crushed itself out of existence.

The effect on the body of an astronaut approaching the center of a black hole would be horrific. The gravitational acceleration, even on the various separate parts of the body, would differ by several million times

49

from that at the surface of Earth—like a tidal force— and in a fraction of a second would rip apart not only the astronaut, but also the molecules and even the atoms of which his organs were composed.

Some scientists believe that gigantic black holes could be at the centers of galaxies, causing them to gather together in clusters as they do. Otherwise, it is argued, why are the stars not scattered evenly throughout the universe, as one would expect them to be?

Only in recent years has man come to realize that the sun that created, warmed, and cherished him for so long is, apart from himself, his one real source of potential destruction; that the glowing monster that feeds us our energy might one day go berserk. Should this happen, it will be the one power against which man is utterly helpless.

Four million tons of the sun's mass is flung off into space as energy every second—energy which bathes the entire solar system and of which tiny Earth receives only a two-billionth part.

To get some idea of its intense power, sensors aboard NASA's orbiting solar observatory in the summer of 1972 reported a vast storm on the sun; it disrupted communications and affected power systems around the world. Recordings taken by the University of New Hampshire showed that energy released by the storm in one hour was equal to the entire United States' electrical-power consumption for a hundred million years at the present rate of use. Imagine, then, the fury of a sun that suddenly gets out of control in a way Perseus's could have done centuries ago.

The majestic death cycle of a star is no less awesome than its birth. Some five thousand million years ago the sun—like Gamma Persei and all the rest of the 130,000 million twinkling stars in our galaxy alone— was conceived in a sensuous, swirling mass of plasma through a galactic intercourse of the elements. It was born, in all its power and glory, to take its destined place in the universe—soon to produce vibrant little offspring of its own in the form of planets, bustling around it on invisible umbilical cords that scientists call gravity.

Some of those offspring—like Earth and Perseus 1—would spend their restless childhood at the mercy of the searing radiation from their mother star. They would then evolve their own means of protection. As clouds formed to temper the blistering fire of mother love, their hot, supple little bodies would writhe and crumple into the turbulent features of adolescence as they began to cool down. The rains would bathe them for centuries. Their birthmarks would fill up with water to become oceans. And, as the radiation of their ever-vigilant parent pumped more energy into the chemicals that formed in the oceans, the molecules of organic life would begin to take shape.

We shall take it that the pattern of life growth on Perseus 1 took place as it did on Earth. Here, a remarkable process known as *photosynthesis* enabled bacteria and algae to transform light energy into carbohydrates, upon which all things feed. Primitive sea plants took root on shore rocks. Soft little creatures began to wriggle through the water.

After many more centuries—perhaps five hundred million years—fish, the earliest vertebrates, dominated the oceans. Later, their gills transformed into lungs to take in oxygen. Living sea creatures then made massive migrations to land to be provided with their life-sustaining air by the recycling of oxygen through the plants until into this exotic world of challenge, perhaps three million years ago, evolved the very creature who now seems intent on causing its entire contamination and destruction . . . man.

To still maintain—despite our growing knowledge of the vibrant, ever-changing universe—that man is alone and unique is surely illogical arrogance in the

51

extreme. One has only to reflect on our insignificance in the living vastness of space.

Every schoolboy knows Earth is round—or near enough. He knows it orbits the sun like the rest of the planets in the solar system. He has been privileged to watch spring-heeled American astronauts bounding about like party balloons in the slow-motion gravity of the moon—real live pictures from space instead of the crude little comic strips his dad read as a kid.

Incredible how we now accept these ballets from space as almost commonplace. Most of us are still stolidly Earthbound in our conceptions. The news of next year's automobile models makes far greater impact than NASA's next probe into the unknown. The average man shrugged at the news that damaged sections of *Skylab* in the summer of 1973 might have left its crew in space for eternity. "The scientists are sure to straighten it out," he said, and turned to the sports pages. And yet a week or so later when two Britons became trapped a few hundred feet beneath the sea in a minisubmarine, the world held its breath and the press splashed the story for every moment of the drama.

Our schoolboy of the seventies finds it hard to believe that back in but a brief moment of time by evolutionary reckoning, even the greatest philosophers of the day were firmly convinced that our wonderful world was as flat as a pancake; the stars just pin pricks in a canopy of blue that enveloped Earth—and only Earth.

Earth was the center of space and man was the ruler of all he surveyed. There was heaven and there was Earth. And that was it. The entire visible wonders of the sun, moon and stars were there for no other reason than to provide man with the light and warmth he needed.

Imagine man's reaction in those early days if someone had come along and presented him with these facts: Earth is a smallish planet orbiting a smallish sun ninety-three million miles away. The sun is one of

130,000 million other suns in a galaxy called the Milky Way. Our galaxy is but one of another hundred thousand million more known galaxies—each with a hundred thousand million more suns!

And those figures are based only on the limit to which our present observation equipment is capable of exploring the universe—and we are still only on the fringe.

Early man thought that the sun was a fraction of the size of the mighty Earth on which he stood. The moon —so friendly, big, and yellow—seemed almost close enough to touch with an outstretched hand. But when he was able to look through telescopes and found that while some of those twinkling "stars" became spheres the planets and other equally bright ones still remained nothing more than pin pricks, he realized that the distances between them were vast.

Today the massive two-hundred-inch eye of Mount Palomar observatory, when trained on one tiny section of the sky, will produce a picture peppered— like diamonds on black velvet—with stars as numerous as a spoonful of granulated sugar. And the giant saucers of our radio telescopes are probing deeper and deeper through the dust and gas clouds that obscure even the heart of our own galaxy from direct vision.

Now, by breaking down and studying the spectra of light emitted by some of these distant stars, we are able to discover what they are made of, their movements, their temperatures, and other characteristics that are giving scientists vital, ever-changing, and ever-increasing information about the restless history of space.

There are giant stars and there are dwarfs. There are those that are constant, reliable, and well behaved. Fortunately for us, our dwarf sun is one of them—a perfectly installed solar central-heating system, thermostatically controlled for us by nature through the many millions of years. There are others—unruly, undisciplined, unpredictable—that at any moment can erupt into the terrifying anger of nova explosion.

Those who blithely talk of man's courageous moon walkabouts as "conquering space" should consider these comparisons: The moon is 240,000 miles away from Earth. Earth is ninety-three million miles from the sun. The sun is twenty-four trillion miles from the nearest star. And for a ray of light to reach us from some of the distant stars—still within our own friendly neighborhood galaxy—takes twenty thousand years traveling at 186,000 miles a second!

It is really quite beyond the human mind to grasp such enormous distances. But to get some idea, let us suppose that the sun is only one yard away from us; the nearest star would be about 120 miles away and the moon about the distance covered by the stride of an ant.

In fact, because of these vast distances, by gazing into our sky at night we are really looking into the past. The light we see left the distant stars thousands of years ago. By now, many of them are extinct. They're not really there at all—we are merely seeing the light, still on its mammoth journey to Earth. Even light from the nearest star, Proxima Centauri, takes just over four years to reach us, compared with eight minutes from the sun.

Astronomers have graded stars according to their magnitude of brightness. The first-magnitude stars are the most brilliant, second-magnitude stars slightly less bright, until we get to the sixth magnitude—a hundred times dimmer than those of the first. We can see up to twenty-five hundred stars with the naked eye, and thousands of millions with the largest telescopes.

As long ago as 400 B.C. the Greek philosopher Democritus was incredibly ahead of his time. He evolved an atomic theory: All matter was composed of tiny particles, too small to be seen. Earth was a swirling mass of atoms, and countless other worlds in space must be evolving just like ours. How close to the scientific evidence we now have—and yet it was expounded to a startled nation nearly twenty-four hundred years ago.

The idea of an atom resembling a solar system with the nucleus as the sun at its center was developed by Niels Bohr, a Danish scientist. Around this core, like planets around a sun, negative-charged particles, called *electrons*, spin in orbit—held away from the central positive nucleus by the force of their negative charges. And each makes a hundred million billion circuits per second!

Yet the source of an atom's power—the nucleus—is so tiny that if the atom were the size of a baseball field, the nucleus would be much smaller than the ball. But it still accounts for very nearly the whole weight of the atom. In fact, a nucleus the size of that mini-baseball would weigh five hundred million tons.

Only during the last fifty years have scientists broken down the nucleus and discovered even smaller particles. And still the search for the ultimate components of matter continues.

It is incredible to think that when certain nuclei are split, the energy given off by the nuclear force that keeps the nucleus together can set off a chain reaction for a bomb that could end civilization as we know it, if used on a mass scale. With the exploding of the first thermonuclear bomb (the hydrogen bomb) in 1952 by triggering off heat intense enough to fuse hydrogen into helium, man was reproducing the energy generated by the sun.

It is quite simple to associate atoms with solar systems. The sun is the proton around which spin the planets (electrons). The systems are the same. Only size and distance, according to our conception of them, are different. A group of atoms forms a particle of matter just as a group of solar systems forms a galaxy of stars. Taken further, a group of particles forms a human being, as a group of galaxies becomes a universe. So man himself is his own universe. It's all simply a matter of relativity.

To man, everything is relative to himself. His size, his strength, his reasoning. To an ant everything is relative to an ant. If a human being were reduced to the size of an ant, a grasshopper would become a dinosaur.

Inversely, had some factional diversity occurred at that vital moment in galactic history when Earth was created, producing instead a body ten times more massive than our modest little planet, man could well have evolved into a flat, lumbering, slothlike creature, struggling to move against the massive pull of his giant world's gravity. It would have taken only some slight malformity of birth for this land of ours to have produced monsters or microbes.

Nearly two thousand years ago the Roman poet Lucretius wrote: "It is in the highest degree unlikely that this earth is the only one to have been created . . . you are bound, therefore, to acknowledge that in other regions there are other earths and various tribes of men and breeds of beasts." Who has really been able to argue with him since? For all life must originate in the same way, wherever it might be found.

Many of the world's top astronomers, astrophysicists, and biologists are now convinced, more than ever before, that there *is* someone out there. Millions of someones. The more we learn about the origin of man, the more we explore the origins of the living universe, the more convincing it becomes that there are many other worlds about us.

That is why scientists are anxiously waiting for that one real proof—a signal, an echo, a flash of light, or a radio pulse that could be the heartbeat of another race desperately trying to make us aware of its existence.

And that race could be the Perseans.

THREE

SPACESHIP EARTH

The time cannot be far off when man will be making his first real attempts to visit other worlds. Already our first steps into space have developed into a lively trot. Up to 1973, only sixteen years after Sputnik 1, sixty-three men had flown in space, twelve had trampled the surface of the moon, and twenty-four had flown around it. *Pioneer 10* has reconnaissanced the surface of Jupiter, 511 million miles from Earth. By the end of this century our space pioneers should have visited the first of our sister planets, probably Mars.

In December 1973 the world gasped when a man-made craft finally shattered the space barrier by actually leaving our own back yard—the solar system. *Pioneer 10*—a messenger from Earth—was on its way to the territory of the alien, never to return.

And before its signals cease to be within the range of our scientists, its delicate equipment will throb with vital new information from space.

Already it has survived the radiation hazards of mighty Jupiter to probe the secrets of this angry planet —secrets that have been hidden since the birth of mankind.

As it hurtled within eighty thousand miles of this glowing, gaseous ball—thirteen hundred times bigger than Earth and more than five hundred million miles away—its signals took forty-five minutes to reach NASA's space listeners. But from them came man's first close-up exploration of the most massive planet in our solar system . . . color photographs and vast amounts of scientific data.

He saw the colorful cloud bands of ammonia, measured the radiation belts and temperatures, tested the magnetic field and the composition of its atmosphere . . . gathered together information that might even give fresh clues on the mystery of how the universe was born.

And as the mighty gravitational force of this solar monster catapulted man's tiny investigator far out into space—as a lacrosse racket sweeps away a ball— it meant that for the first time man could be sending proof of his existence to alien worlds.

And it is a territory we *must* explore. . . .

Our cozy way of life on Earth could well be seriously threatened over the next fifty years. We are overloading it with people, burning up its energy far too recklessly, polluting its crops and vital organic life. In fact, making too many aimless demands on its generosity. We're slowly killing this great big golden goose of ours. And, for the sake of generations still to come, we must start *now* on the most gigantic overspill scheme in our history—the selecting of other planetary homes where man could survive—together with an all-out technological drive to produce the means of getting him there.

Every new challenge seems to produce a special breed of invincible men and women dedicated to meet it. And this new generation of space explorers may well break the international barriers of politics and prejudice, drawing nations together so that we shall no longer challenge each other, but pool our thoughts and resources to meet the one challenge that really matters —the survival of mankind.

In 1975 we may see the first evidence of this—an American-Soviet handshake in space, with the docking of their orbiting satellites. And even if new techniques, and more orderly social and economic policies enable us to remain here on Earth, equipping our scientists to share the secrets awaiting them in the infinite laboratory of the universe could mean a new and better life for generations to come. Many spin-off benefits have already resulted from NASA's space programs over recent years in such fields as medicine, communication, and data processing. Interstellar flight—and, more particularly, contact with extraterrestrial life—could mean unlimited advances in our culture.

It is rather significant that the estimated world population at this time is 4,500 million—which works out at precisely one person per year of Earth's existence (4,500 million years). It might therefore be prudent to maintain these comparisons as a limiting factor to population growth and the flexibility of Earth's resources. It seems quite obvious that if we continue our present extravagance we shall—like Perseus 1—be searching for new worlds far sooner than we think.

Just how serious are the current threats to our survival? . . .

A great deal of controversy arose following the publication in 1971 of a startling report by the Massachusetts Institute of Technology. Their computerizing of variable factors such as population, food supplies, natural resources, and pollution resulted in fearsome predictions that global disaster was inevitable within the next hundred years.

The research was sponsored by an international group of scientists, industrialists, economists, and others concerned with the "predicament of mankind."

It indicated catastrophic pollution leading to famine and thousands of millions of deaths. And Professor Dennis L. Meadows, who headed the MIT project, believes the computer forecasts are already coming true with the world's food and energy crises. "Between ten and thirty million people will starve to death in 1974," he is reported as forecasting.

However, Thomas J. Boyle of the Lowell Observatory at Flagstaff, Arizona, writing in the scientific journal *Nature* in 1973, claimed that the original computer programming contained a "typographical error" which, when corrected, would give quite different results. In fact, he said, it would show that a stable and prosperous world may be reached by the year 2100.

But whether or not the MIT computers miscalculated, many eminent scientists are deeply concerned about our abuse of our generous planet. They maintain that projects like *Skylab*, NASA's wide-ranging space laboratory launched in 1973, with its highly sensitive multispectral scanning system, will be vital in the location of desperately needed information on crop growth, mineral deposits, and atmosphere pollution in the battle to preserve our precious supplies.

Professor Wernher von Braun, America's top space authority and one of the masterminds of the Apollo Moonshot program, compares our tiny, overcrowded world to a solitary spaceship on which 4,500 million astronauts are aimlessly journeying to an unknown destination. This spaceship, he says, has onboard a strictly limited supply of raw materials on which its astronauts—you and I—must exist.

And yet we are all abusing this supply in a way that seems to mean we have only one aim—to exterminate ourselves. "We are, in fact, approaching a global catastrophe, and it is imperative that determined measures are taken at once," says the professor. "If we continue as we are, the starvation and infant mortality rate that is at present limited to local pockets of mankind, will be a widespread phenomenon. There will be wholesale lack of employment because of the absence of raw materials. In places such as India, Bangla Desh, and parts of Brazil, the problem will get completely out of control, causing widespread misery."

Is there yet hope that this overmanned spaceship of ours—with its better-off passengers recklessly wasting and polluting vast proportions of its supplies while so many "tourist class" travelers are wiped out by disease and malnutrition—can still survive? To do so we must gain a better understanding of supply and demand patterns by means of a well-organized global marketing system. More satellites must be used to give reliable data in all countries on the availability of mineral and food resources, population density, growth of cities, and levels of pollution. These findings must then be fed through computers to tell us what must go where before famine overcomes a nation. And, insist the scientists, population growth must be checked.

Plans are already being made for a satellite to be launched in 1975 to beam family-planning programs to remote villagers watching communal television sets in India.

"Only One Earth"—a special report commissioned by the Secretary General of the United Nations Conference on the Human Environment, prepared with the assistance of a committee of 152 consultants in fifty-eight countries and published in 1972—says:

"We are indeed travelers bound to Earth's crust, drawing life from the air and water of its thin and fragile envelope, using and reusing its very limited supply of natural resources. The fundamental task of the UN Conference is to formulate the problems inherent in the limitations of Spaceship Earth, and to devise patterns of collective behavior compatible with the continued flowering of civilizations."

And it presents this grim description of man's environment:

"The actual life of most of mankind has been

61

cramped with back-breaking labor, exposed to deadly or debilitating disease, prey to wars and famines, haunted by the loss of children, filled with fear and the ignorance that breeds more fear. At the end, for everyone, stands dreaded unknown death."

How much longer can our precious resources last?

Experts forecast that demands on electrical forms of energy alone will increase three hundred to four hundred percent in the next twenty years. Sources of iron ore may soon be desperately short. There is already a world oil crisis, and automobile ownership on anything like the present scale cannot exist in the next century.

There seems little doubt that even before the 1980s most aspects of normal social life will have to be adjusted to cope with the growing energy crisis. Fuel rationing, whether voluntary or government imposed, seems bound to be a feature of Western life. Americans alone use up about thirty-five percent of the world's energy. That proportion must drop drastically as developing nations demand a greater share.

The long-term answer may well lie in our ability to draw our supplies directly from the sun. It is continuous and bountiful—there for the taking, if we can evolve an economically feasible method of getting at it. Unfortunately, the land area needed to collect enough radiation for industrial needs would be vast, as would the conversion and storage systems. But it is a concept our scientists must exploit.

Meanwhile, one thing is certain. We cannot possibly continue to haphazardly waste power as we do today. We might even have to slow things down a little. It has been estimated that when an automobile is produced in Detroit, eighty percent of the total energy expended in the entire process is wasted because of the excessively high speed at which it is run off the assembly line. And the energy needed for each transworld air traveler is forty times more than that required by someone taking a slow boat from Europe to China.

In 1973 Americans suddenly became aware that an energy crisis really does exist. By the latter half of the year motorists in Boston were being urged to join a "commuter computer" system which paired strangers so that they could pool their cars. Seattle was offering free bus services to private-car users and the big sales pitch from many automobile manufacturers was "increased fuel economy." Oil companies too were urging motorists to ease up on the accelerator. Some European countries banned Sunday motoring altogether.

Faced with worldwide oil and coal crises, the biggest fuel question of the century is: Do we go all-out for nuclear power with vast, unrestrained chains of mighty breeder reactors to feed the world's energy consumers, who grow more gluttonous every day? There appears to be no doubt that uranium-fed reactors could satisfy the world's mounting appetite for the next hundred years, after which fusion reactors could take over.

It has been estimated that the average person now uses one kilowatt of energy per year and that there are something like 4,500 million people in the world. That makes a total requirement of 4,500 million kilowatts. Let us assume that by the turn of the century the population trebles and energy requirements increase to ten kilowatts per person. The energy required would, therefore, be 135,000 million kilowatts. As each metric ton of natural uranium provides 140 kilowatts per year, a stock of a hundred million metric tons of uranium would provide the world's energy for more than a century, using the basic type of fission reactors in most present-day nuclear power plants. And there appears to be no shortage of uranium, a ton of which gives the power output of twenty thousand tons of coal.

It has been estimated that uranium in the Earth's crust totals some hundred million million metric tons, with more than two percent of it within a mile of the surface. It would only require a small fraction of this two percent to provide that hundred million tons needed to supply energy for a hundred years to a population much larger and more extravagant than at present. And, if breeder reactors were used—in which fuel is recycled time and time again—only one-tenth of the natural uranium would be needed.

But can all this latent power be safely contained? Can we be sure that its lethal waste, which can remain radioactive for thousands of years, will not seep out of captivity and into our bodies, or explode with all the fury of a nuclear bomb? During an Atomic Energy Commission survey it was estimated that if one of our current standard-type reactors exploded, it would devastate an area the size of Pennsylvania and slaughter forty-five thousand people, either immediately or through the slow, agonizing death from radiation sickness.

Perhaps one of the greatest causes for concern is the control of the vast quantities of fissile material when the waste products are being processed. This processing results in fresh plutonium, which can be used as fuel by itself in fast reactors, or mixed with uranium in low breeder reactors.

By the middle of the next century we shall be processing between 1.5 and 2 million metric tons of uranium annually. Although the plutonium required to make a nuclear weapon would not be of precisely the same form, the further processing required will soon be within the technical capability of several nations.

Only a few kilograms of plutonium, or U235, are needed to make a relatively simple weapon with a yield of ten to twenty kilotons of TNT—similar to the bombs first used on Nagasaki and Hiroshima. The nuclear nations will therefore need to precisely monitor down to one part in ten billion exactly what happens to this deadly material throughout its processing to be sure that plutonium is not being secretly removed and taken out of the country.

In her book *Food in History* authoress Reay Tannahill foresees us all collecting our lunches from a factory production line with synthetic beef made from fuel oil and bacon from an extract of algae. The days of the T-bone steak could well be numbered. Scientists have already produced a variety of edible manmade fibers which may, in the not-too-distant future, replace many of our dwindling natural food supplies. A firm in Britain has produced chicken- and beef-flavored chunks, spun from protein of the common field bean, which can be served as tasty cutlets, meatballs, and many other dishes.

Most of the pampered Western world is at last becoming aware that an abundant, never-ending supply of food may not always be around for the taking.

Other food experts believe we may eventually be forced to breed alternative forms of farm animals that would require less feeding than traditional cattle. We may well find such items as zebra steaks and snake rissoles on our everyday menu.

However, a drastic reduction in the gluttonous food intake of the Western world would be acceptable to most nutritionists. It would be the one real answer to beat the national bulge and to get us all down to a healthy weight. In December 1972 nutritionist Dr. D. A. Hems of Imperial College, London, told a seminar that Britons were more than a hundred thousand tons overweight. "The problem of obesity," he said, "is enormous. At least one British adult in six is overweight. Few animal species indulge in such corporate abuse."

But even with stricter economy of food and fuel supplies, overcrowding may still one day force us to move out of our solar system in search of other suitable worlds.

The population of the United States took 150 years to reach its first hundred million. The next hundred million took fifty years, and if the average family has three children, the next hundred million will take only twenty-five years. And so on and so on, until the result becomes astronomical.

This is what is happening to one developed nation, one that is able to produce and afford the medical and scientific know-how to keep its nation alive and fit longer. It is ironic that the mere process of keeping us alive longer could be one of the factors in bringing about our eventual self-destruction through lack of space and resources. Consider, for instance, the fact that each one of those extra new American babies will need an estimated million calories of food per year for probably ten and maybe thirty years longer than its parents.

Hoyle put the population explosion in a very significant way when he said that if the present rate continues, within five thousand years the total mass of humanity will exceed the mass of all the planets, stars, and galaxies visible with the two-hundred-inch telescope on Mount Palomar.

The world population—around four hundred million in Roman times—reached its first thousand million in the sixteenth to seventeenth centuries. It doubled by the year 1900, after only three hundred years, and trebled after only a further fifty years. By the end of the century seven billion people could be grasping for a share of the world's resources. Professor Henry Kahn of Hudson Research Institute has estimated the total could "top out" at fifteen thousand million to thirty thousand million!

This situation in itself could begin to stimulate preliminary searches for an overspill world in our galaxy.

FOUR

SEARCH AMONG THE STARS

Let us presume it is now 950 A.D. on the planet Perseus 1. During the fifty years since those first foreboding hints of its impending destruction, its astronomers, astrophysicists and biologists would have gathered far more accurate information about the length of time their people could safely remain on the planet.

Lowest estimates might have been around 250 years. A century before that, dramatic changes in climate and temperature would have overcome many of them—despite the special protection that would have been devised to temper their sun's increasing radiation.

But the first major question their scientists would have had to answer must have been: Where were the new worlds outside their dying solar system to which they could eventually escape? Which of the millions that winked invitingly from the crowded skies about them could really offer suitable refuge for their future emigrants into space?

67

To find them they would have had to begin mass exploration of the universe on a scale far vaster, far more intensive than ever before, though even at their existing stage of astronomical research they would have possessed a far wider understanding of other star systems then we have now.

To get some idea of the enormity of this urgent new rummage among the stars, let's consider the problem in the light of man's present knowledge of the universe.

To start with, how many stars are there out there, and how many of them might conceivably support life as we know it? No one, of course, has any real idea. But estimates from current research are that there could be something like 10^{28} *observable* stars in the universe. There must be many more, but we are not able to see them due to the curvature of light and the infinite depth of the universe. But for a moment stop and consider that figure of 10^{28} (ten to the power of twenty-eight). That means 100,000,000,000,000,000,-000,000,000,000 heavenly bodies that seem to us no more than tiny, flickering fireflies in the night and yet can be millions of times brighter than our own blazing sun.

So to keep things to comprehensible proportions, let's simply consider the 135,000 million stars in our own galaxy, the Milky Way. From this still-massive total, only certain of them can be seriously considered as possible supporters of our kind of life. Firstly, only those that remain active for a long period of time (our sun is five thousand million years old) would give life its chance to evolve as we have.

Secondly, the majority of stars are either in pairs or groups which might cause so much gravitational confusion for their orbiting planets that conditions on them would probably be too unsettled for life to get started.

And thirdly, planets would need to be of medium size. One too small, say the size of our moon, might be unable to hold an atmosphere long enough for initial biological evolution. Alternatively, the powerful gravity of a giant planet would not allow its primitive hydrogen and hydrocarbon atmosphere to escape in time for life to develop beyond its simplest forms—though, of course, biochemical systems different from our own might survive.

And so, taking all these requirements into account, it has been estimated that only two percent of double or multiple stars could have habitable planets, and ten percent of single stars—which still leaves plenty of possible candidates. Five thousand million, in fact. And even if only one in a thousand of these has the correct chemical requirements to produce life, there still remains a formidable choice of five million suns with planets where extraterrestrial civilizations might exist. Remember too that our entire galaxy is only one of a hundred thousand million more galaxies in the known universe!

It is now generally accepted that Earth life began by the interaction of various inanimate chemicals. And many times over the last twenty years this process has been simulated in laboratory conditions such as are thought to have existed on Earth in primitive times.

Quite simply, a gas mixture of methane and ammonia over water is subjected to energy sources, such as the sun, radiation, etc., at levels and intensities believed to have been prevalent in those early days. When the products of these reactions were analyzed, they were found to contain the biochemicals required in our bodies as part of our metabolic process. It is therefore logical to say that, given similar conditions and chemicals, there is no reason why the same life-producing reactions should not be taking place elsewhere in the universe.

How can we tell when a star has planets? We can't see them even with our largest telescopes due to their vast distances from us and because they become lost in the glare of their sun. But giant planets of stars up to about fifty light-years away are being discovered because their powerful gravitational force can actually make their parent star "wobble" as it is being orbited. So, if we detect a wobble, there's probably a planet somewhere around.

One of the most significant advances in detecting the structure of space began in the late nineteenth century, when light from stars began to be analyzed by its spectra. At Harvard some ten thousand stars were classified. Seventy years later the list had reached 360,000.

These spectral analyses revealed, among other things, temperature variations. The hottest showed spectral readings for highly ionized helium, nitrogen, and silicon. They were classified by the letter W. The coolest stars were given the letter S. So now the full range, in order of decreasing temperature, is listed as follows: W,O,B,-A,F,G,K,M,R,N,S—conveniently remembered by students of astronomy through the immortal phrase "Wow! Oh Be A Fine Girl, Kiss Me Right Now Sweetheart!"

It was also discovered that the heavier the star, the hotter and brighter it was. However, big stars burn their hydrogen so fast that they can preserve life for perhaps as little as only a million years—far too short a time for advanced life to evolve. Earth is estimated to be 4.6 billion years old, and about a third of that time was required for the evolution of the chemicals which finally produced what we accept as a life form.

The small (M) stars could remain for a hundred billion years, but the drawback with these is that their output of energy is so feeble that only a narrow zone around them would have a suitable temperature range. Therefore it is the moderate stars—the F,G, and K types—that are most likely candidates. Our own sun is a G-type star.

F stars are quite likely to have evolved intelligent life at a more rapid rate. Their radiation would be more intense and likely to "stir the primordial soup" more quickly. We would therefore expect such devel-

70

opments as interstellar travel to come from these star systems.

Scientists now consider that virtually all single stars have planets. The nearest known single star is Barnard's—a faint red dwarf—discovered in 1916 by Edward E. Barnard. By 1956 astronomers were almost certain that Barnard's star had a planet orbiting it, and this was finally confirmed in 1963 by the American Astronomical Society. Since then, Peter Van de Kamp of Sproul University in Pennsylvania announced that Barnard's star has two planets and, more recently, researchers at NASA state that it could have three giant ones, like our own Jupiter, Saturn, and Uranus. Some other stars believed to have planets are listed in Appendix 2.

There is now sound scientific reason to believe that life may occupy thousands of planets within our own galaxy alone. The setting up of earth-orbiting observatories free from the disconcerting effects of our atmosphere, or on a site such as the moon, should reveal immense new knowledge of our cosmic neighbors.

But until man is able to conquer interstellar travel, his search for extraterrestrial intelligences must continue through a global network of radio astronomical space searches—not only for messages that might be specifically directed at Earth, but for the many stray signals being transmitted between other planets in the galaxy.

For if one accepts that other races exist—and that a vast number of them are far more advanced than ourselves—one must also assume that many are in frequent communication with each other, exchanging knowledge and passing on vital information through the universal stepping stones of hosts of interplanetary transmitting and receiving bases.

It is, of course, indicative of man's supreme arrogance for him to assume that whoever *is* out there *must* wish to contact him. But why should they? Why should they spend more time on us than on the thousands of other inhabited worlds of which they are most likely aware? If our radio ears are not cocked when they call, they'll probably be far too busy doing their interstellar rounds to hang about just in case we happen to put out the right signal.

And remember too that many of them could have been putting calls into us for thousands of years. They could well be excused for assuming we're still sending messages by carrier pigeon.

Soviet scientist N. S. Kardashev segregates extraterrestrial societies into three grades (types I, II, and III) according to the advanced stage of their technology. Type I societies would seem the most likely to be interested in contacting Earth, but unfortunately may, like ourselves, require much more elaborate communication systems than presently exist. Carl Sagan advocates that we give more serious attention to the supercivilizations (types II and III) who would be more equipped to harness the power to reach us by "antique" communication methods we could comprehend, like radio.

In a rather ego-shattering theory he calls the Zoo Hypothesis, John A. Ball, a Harvard student from Massachusetts writing in a 1973 issue of the journal *Icarus*, suggests that some superior aliens are deliberately avoiding contact with us and have, instead, set aside the area in which we live as a zoo! That they merely want to observe us without being identified— something they would have the technological know-how to ensure. We would, in fact, be an interstellar conservation area!

Of all the possible radio wavelength frequencies available to choose from, how can we pick the right one being used by an extraterrestrial transmitter? Of course, we can't. But we can apply a little bit of the old Sherlock Holmes logic.

Suppose that you'd arranged to meet a colleague at a certain time in New York City, but for some reason forgot to nominate the precise spot. It would be quite out of the question to search the entire city. What would Holmes do? He would probably decide which was the best-known place in the city, like Central Park, assuming that his friend, Dr. Watson, would use the same logic.

This is exactly the logic a radio astronomer would be expected to use. In other words, to listen or transmit on the frequency associated with something universally familiar. And an obvious choice would be twenty-one centimeters, because hydrogen—the most common element in the universe—emits radio pulses at this frequency. This, therefore, might well be the most obvious "interstellar rendezvous" any intelligence would be likely to select.

There is, however, one reason why an emerging civilization may *not* wish to use twenty-one centimeters: even if this is a universally recognized wavelength, they may feel it is too vital to their physicists in the study of natural signals to clutter it up with artificial ones.

Precisely this problem has occurred on Earth, where commercial radio activity made it extremely difficult for our astronomers to use the twenty-one centimeters line in their search for natural and, possibly, artificial signals. Fortunately, common sense has prevailed, and an agreed gap has been left clear on either side of the twenty-one centimeters line to allow the astronomers to work in peace, without continual interference from other radio transmitters.

Some scientists suggest we use 10.5 centimeters, which is twice the frequency and half the wavelength of the 21-centimeters line. And there are other "universal frequencies" that might be tried, such as 18 centimeters, which corresponds to the natural signals from water vapor, and 0.4 centimeters from formaldehyde (a compound similar to life-forming complexes).

In fact, to stand any real chance of hitting on that

73

same interstellar rendezvous with another intelligence, it will be necessary to try our luck on several wave bands . . . just as Holmes and his endearing doctor would have certainly increased the odds of finding each other by trying not only Central Park, but Fifth Avenue, the Tivoli, Carnegie Hall, and Grand Central Station too. As Holmes would remark—"It's elementary, my dear Watson."

How wide a range would the Perseans' heavenly reconnaissance need to cover? At a distance of a hundred light-years from their planet, there might be something like a thousand life-bearing stars. To reach out another hundred light-years could offer them a choice of around ten thousand stars. At a thousand light-years away from home there could be many millions. However, a likely search would be over two hundred light-years. This would, of course, bring Earth well within the range.

They would be looking for stars in the F, G, K, and possibly M range, with planets large enough for the gravity to retain oxygen in its atmosphere, but small enough to allow the release of hydrogen. A satisfactory size for the evolution of advanced life would be from one thousand to twenty thousand kilometers radius. The radius of Earth is about 6,380 kilometers.

FIVE

THE ELECTRONIC MIND

On a planet such as Perseus, threatened by a dying sun, only a vast and sophisticated technology could save it from extinction. How would their technology have achieved such an advanced state?

Every scrap of data gathered by the Perseans' massive radio telescopes and other astronomical equipment as they scanned the skies for new star systems would have been fed into a vast computer complex.

This is where all major analysis would have been handled for many years. For on a planet as technologically advanced as this, the mathematical logic of the computer would have long since taken over the menial administration from the highly sensitive Perseans.

They would have accepted the situation and, after many years of trial, error, and near disaster, would have learned to live profitably with the mechanical intellects of their own conception.

The precarious system of government by living

representatives, with all its frailties, indecision, emotional and inconsistent policies, would have long been abandoned. The bickering, the fears, jealousies, ambitions, and the greed of their ancient heads of state led them all into catastrophic wars, polluted their precious atmosphere almost to a point of extinguishing life, and dragged them through the suffering, hunger, and degradation of a totally unbalanced and selfish society.

Only with the advent of its one world computer center, with its orderly, entirely rational, and predictable system of automated government, would their race have begun to reorganize the dwindling resources of their planet fairly and without waste; distribute its wealth, food, and energy with scientific efficiency so that all could share.

Where would have been the living leader who could have restrained his inherent prejudice, conceit, and ambition sufficiently to bring about such things? For generations now all major decisions on national policy would have been made by the central computer-brain complex. And so to this same unbiased intelligence they would now have turned with the most dramatic crisis in their long history . . . how to survive.

To us here on Earth, the suggestion that the human mind might one day be dominated by a mechanical substitute is repulsive. Like some nightmare theme for a cheap science fiction comic of the 1930s. And yet, after only a quarter of a century, electronic computers are surreptitiously and increasingly infiltrating our daily lives.

They demand our money, they diagnose our health, they tell us how many children we should produce, how many cigarettes we should smoke. They can hire us and fire us. They can beat us at chess. They can gobble up all our little secrets and spew them out as evidence against us for the debt collectors, government officials, and civil servants.

Our precious lives are entrusted to their metallic logic as they increasingly take over our airports, railways, and first timid steps into space. They could annihilate us altogether by their cold, merciless calculations in a nuclear war.

And, frightening though it may seem, these artificial organisms could, like the first tiny life forms that began to evolve on primitive Earth those millions of years ago, advance even more rapidly and relentlessly into mechanisms of greater and greater complexity. If we compare, as we must, even our most advanced computers of the 1970s with the amoeba's place in the evolution of human life, consider what awesome influence computers will wield when, like man, they become fully developed.

How much more will they be controlling us—even another twenty-five years from now? A great deal of study is going on now throughout the world to bring the computer even more intimately into our personal way of life. Scientists at Stanford University in California are researching the possibilities of constructing a computer to which any layman could give verbal instructions from which it would perform tasks. It would even be programmed to understand all types of voice patterns. The scientists also want computers to "see" objects and recognize situations, clarify them, and work with them by using their own artificial intelligence.

A paper by D. F. Lawden, professor of mathematical physics at Aston University in England, points out that the general opinion of most scientists is that "the phenomenon of consciousness can be completely comprehended in terms of the behavior of a physical system: Thus, a computer constructed entirely from transistors and other electronic components and programmed to behave in a human manner, including the initiation of original patterns of thought, is, according to this view, *conscious*, and no other meaning is attached to this term."

Already the electronic amoeba is going through its

first alarming population explosion, with its production rate approximately doubling every year.

Will *we* finally allow them to take us over, as they would have almost done on Perseus? Can we, in fact, still stop them from reaching such an overwhelming complexity of permutative perfection that will eventually enable them to think and to make their own decisions? For even now a computer can be trained to program itself and seek out its own ways to solve a set problem.

Basically, the mechanics of its "brain" follow the pattern of a man's. Its eye is the tape reader that scans the data before it. True, it has to be programmed initially by humans before it can pump out its information. But aren't we all programmed from the moment dad tells us the simple facts of life, through the years of fact-and-figure pounding we get at school and through books, press, television, and other media up until the moment we die? And just like the stored-up items in the memory bank of a computer, the things we were told as children stay with us to influence our entire adult thinking. How many of us are still scared of the dark because that early programming included tales of ghosts, witches, and child-gobbling ogres?

Thinking can be defined as the ability to interpret the results of a mental investigation or enquiry and to act accordingly. A computer does precisely this. Granted, with even our most up-to-date equipment, the amount of time required to search through its memory bank for one particular item of data is incredibly greater than that required by man. The human brain—with its ten million million neurons, or "information elements," takes about a tenth of a second. And yet to arrive at that item for recall, it must perform something like a hundred thousand operations, for the human memory is estimated to contain some one thousand million stored-up patterns.

A computer capable of ten million operations per second would take one-hundredth of a second to check each of those thousand million patterns, making a total of 110 days—or four months for a complete matching check which takes the human brain one-tenth of a second.

But, as we've said, the twentieth-century computer is only a crude prototype of the almost magical systems that must eventually be developed. Already a quarter of a million "units of logic," each containing the equivalent of twenty-two electronic components, can be packed into the space of one cubic inch.

It cannot be long before we have computers the size of human brains. How long, then, before they will have the ability to disregard programming, rearrange their set patterns of mechanical logic, and act independently of man's instructions? Once this situation arises, what can stop them from communicating with each other in codes indecipherable to man; of virtually taking over the establishment?

Whatever the outcome here on Earth, it is obvious we must either strangle mass computerization in its comparatively puny childhood or learn to live with it in a manner that will benefit us rather than destroy our self-respect and stifle our creativeness.

Many observers believe that man is deteriorating both mentally and physically despite the gigantic strides in technology, and that the unfit are being kept alive by medical science to reproduce more weak descendants, making each generation more puny than the one before. In the tough, bad old days, they maintain, only the fittest survived.

There could be a danger very soon that, with electronic brains of greater and greater complexity and automation for virtually all physical tasks, man will no longer be required to think or act for himself.

One British computer expert, Ivor Catt, claims these "mindless monsters" regularly go berserk and ruin the information collated in their memory banks. He even warns that computers controlling the launch of nuclear missiles might one day run riot and precipitate a third world war.

There are, however, some hopeful signs that we shall harness computers for the good of humanity. Millions of people all over the world who are themselves little more than human robots in their jobs are being released to fuller lives by factory automation, and so avoiding that soul-destroying stress that is so prevalent in the assembly-line industries.

Professor Meredith Thring, head of the Department of Mechanical Engineering at the University of London, predicts that we shall have surgery by robot hands and electronic scalpels to meet the demands of increasingly delicate and intricate forms of surgery. Will we eventually have operations programmed and performed entirely mechanically? If so, how many lives might be preserved without those human errors?

Professor Thring is working on other mechanical aids that may make life easier for us all in the future, particularly women. Already he has produced a stair-climbing robot "housewife" and is now working on an advanced version—with robot hands and arms, a TV eye and small electronic brain—that will be able to carry objects up to dustbin-size, cope with washing and cleaning jobs, make beds, set a table, and remember where things came from and put them back. And in Bavaria, Gunter Beltzig has invented what he claims is the first automated cradle. It rocks baby gently to sleep while playing soothing lullabies, warms its bottle, sterilizes diapers and stores food at the right temperature.

Computers might even take over traffic direction from the police. A firm in New York has developed a system in which a mobile minicomputer is taken to the scene of a road accident, where it is fed with such data as the type of vehicles involved, damage, skid marks, and evidence from the drivers and eyewitnesses. This is then processed and transmitted to a central computer which has been programmed to assess the importance and reliability of various items of evidence. It then attempts to reconstruct the accident, and can even indicate traffic-law infractions. The equipment, built with a grant of two hundred thousand dollars from the National Highway Traffic Safety Administration, is to be handed over to police units for field testing in 1976.

One man has produced a computer that can smile, scowl, and move its "mouth" in response to speech. The "face" is a round screen. All the vowels and some consonants can be represented on it by using the computer to vary the shapes of the illuminated outline of a mouth. Inventor David Boston hopes his device will help children to lip-read at the Royal National Institute for the Deaf in London.

In September 1973 the *National Enquirer* newspaper asked some top American computer scientists how soon these mechanical brains would actually outthink man. These were some of their quoted remarks:

Professor Herbert Simon of Carnegie-Mellon University in Pittsburgh, Pennsylvania: "I can't see anything to stop machines from becoming more intelligent than men within one generation. Watch a computer play chess and you realize it thinks the way we do. With more time and effort put into programming I am sure we could come up with a computer to beat world chess champ Bobby Fischer."

Daniel G. Bobrow, principal scientist at the Xerox computer science laboratory in Palo Alto, California: "There's no reason why the computer cannot intellectually surpass its creator."

Computer-science professor Ranon Banerji of Case Western Reserve University, Cleveland, Ohio: "Machines will be so smart it will be a pleasure to have them as friends. They will soon begin to develop their own hunches."

It is fairly obvious that the doctors, surgeons, dieticians, and biologists of a sophisticated society such as the

Perseans' would have evolved methods of greatly increasing the active physical and mental life span of their race. The scientific genius of a contemporary Isaac Newton or Albert Einstein would no longer be restricted by a few-score years. Long after the age at which man now reaches senility, intellects of this caliber would barely have approached their peak.

Many of our own scientists reckon that at the present rate of surgical, medical, and social advancement, and with more balanced dietary control, man's normal life expectancy can be doubled in the twenty-first century. Some even predict a life span of two hundred years. It is likely that most advanced forms of extraterrestrial life will have achieved at least this duration.

It is not so implausible that man should soon reach this stage of mental and physical preservation when one considers how much twentieth-century societies are already outlasting their predecessors. In Imperial Rome life expectancy was twenty-two years. In America, at the end of the last century, it had risen to forty-seven. Today, a baby can expect to reach seventy-five, and there are more centenarians than ever before.

In 1973 Dr. David Davies, a forty-three-year-old lecturer from University College in London, was commissioned by the government of Ecuador to scientifically study the remarkable inhabitants of the hidden valley of Vilcabamba. On a previous visit Dr. Davies brought back evidence of a population where thirty percent of births are given by women over 45, where baptismal certificates record ages up to 150, where the oldest surviving inhabitant is 142 and men still work a full day in the fields at 120.

The local doctor there believes the word of one 120-year-old man who boasts he still makes love to his 92-year-old wife in their little mud-brick hut, and Dr. Davies reports meeting one 64-year-old woman "who looked 34 and had a son of 8."

One of the reasons for the longevity of these five

thousand Vilcabambans—who smoke forty to sixty cigarettes per day and are heavy rum drinkers—is thought to be their low-calorie diet, consisting mainly of fruit and vegetables. They eat only about one ounce of meat per week. High blood pressure, heart disease, and cancer are extremely rare; they never go bald and reach these great ages without losing their teeth, agility, or mental faculties.

Dr. Davies, who is convinced that man's life span should not be limited to less than two hundred years, is now doing much deeper research into the secrets of this happy little Shangri-la in the belief they may help us all to find a new lease on life.

Scientists believe that correct diet alone can give us a twenty-percent increase in life span. Already Dr. Alex Comfort of University College in London has increased the life span of laboratory mice by twelve percent by feeding them food with large amounts of compounds called *antioxidants*. These reduce the level of oxygen activity in the body. Dr. Irene Gore, a researcher who has worked with Dr. Comfort in a study group on aging, told me: "I think it is a distinct possibility, on theoretical grounds, that antioxidants could be used to increase the life span of humans. But at this stage, of course, we have to be cautious even though they do not appear to have had detrimental side-effects on animals."

But the scientists do not merely want to prolong senility. Their aim is to extend our active life by keeping us all feeling about thirty years old when we're actually fifty.

How will society change when we have all extended our life spans by even another twenty or thirty years? Dr. Clive Wood, who teaches contraception at Oxford University in England, makes these interesting predictions in the British magazine *New Scientist:*

Young people will find job hunting and promotion more difficult because the senior staff will be useful to the company for much longer. They will still be vigorous and bursting with ideas. Retirement will have to be made compulsory to give youth a chance. Couples will have their first children much later in life and parenthood will be a feature of retirement rather than the busiest part of a young parent's life. Manual workers will be frustrated by having to be retired in middle age, especially with increased automation, while still full of vitality and energy.

Leisure facilities will barely cope with the growing number of hearty, fun-loving people seeking outlets for their unflagging energies. To sail, play golf, or ride a horse on the weekend will mean queuing on Friday night. And, says Dr. Wood, road traffic conditions scarcely bear thinking about.

There are obviously many other things that would drastically change. More girls would become involved with middle-aged men, who could better afford to look after them. The divorce rate could become astronomical with seventy-year-olds still full of the joys of spring, and football stars still scoring in their sixties.

Sir Richard Doll, a sixty-year-old professor of medicine at Oxford University, says people over sixty-five should "live dangerously, enjoy life to the full, and not mollycoddle themselves." Today, stories of the increasing mental and physical vitality of old people crop up all over the world. In 1973 Charlie Smith, a Florida man who boasted he'd ridden with Jessie James—claimed he was 131.

In the summer of 1973 four thousand spectators at a sports stadium in San Diego, California, cheered eighty-eight-year-old British athlete Duncan Maclean into fourth place in the hundred-meters sprint—which he did in sixteen seconds flat! After the race, this five-foot-three-inch Scotsman (he was nick-named the Tartan Flash because of the material his shorts were made of) told me: "It's all in the mind. You must just make yourself do these things if you want to stay young."

In the same year, after climbing 17,500 feet up

Mount Everest, sixty-four-year-old Elizabeth Foster from England said: "People kept thinking 'that old trout will never get up there'—but I proved them all wrong."

Which fields of medical science are likely to help give us all those hundred, or even two hundred-plus life spans in the future? In September 1973 eleven celebrated scientists and clinicians from various parts of the world contributed their predictions to a symposium on "Medicine in the Twenty-first Century."

Professor J. Englebert Dunphy, chairman of the department of surgery at the University of California, spoke of exciting new concepts of fetal surgery in which defects will be detected and corrected before a baby is born. He foresees greatly increased survival rates in cancer sufferers and many forms of cancer being totally curable, along with substantial advances in neurosurgery, nerve grafting, control of rheumatoid arthritis, and many other complaints that plague present-day mankind.

There will also, he predicts, be incredible advances in the repression of physical suffering at the turn of the century. Simply taking a pill will completely eliminate pain. The scalpel will become obsolete with the advent of a cutting and coagulating current which will divide tissue and seal blood vessels. Already a Colorado firm is producing surgical equipment which uses radio-frequency energy to cut through flesh and to stop bleeding. "However," says Professor Dunphy, "despite spectacular advances in organ transplant, the need will be less because of a general slowing down of the aging process."

Ulf von Euler, professor of physiology at the Karolinska Institute in Stockholm, believes we shall have drugs to precisely control a person's willpower, attitudes, and emotional states. And certainly a do-it-yourself abortion pill.

Electronic pain-killing equipment is already being used in America and Britain. A small implanted radio receiver triggers an electrode attached to a nerve and immediately obliterates pain. Another method now being used involves an hour-long operation in which an electric current is used to kill the spinal nerve which carries pain from the affected part of the body to the brain. The banishment of pain then lasts for two years or more, and doctors using this treatment claim an eighty-five percent success rate.

Artificial eyes and ears seem almost certain to bring a new and exciting world to the blind and the deaf. Research using such techniques as laser beams, plastic corneas, and transplants is already advancing rapidly all over the world.

The time cannot be far off when a completely self-contained artificial eye, controlled by the brain, will be available. British surgeons recently implanted a miniature receiver in a woman's head, then connected it to the sight-controlling mechanism of her brain. When radio signals were beamed at microscopic electrodes beneath the woman's scalp, she saw them as spots of light.

By further development of this system, Professor Giles Brindley of London University believes artificial eyes will, in the next few years, be used in conjunction with miniature TV cameras. These cameras would scan book pages or newspapers and transmit the images, in the form of radio signals, to be picked up by a receiver implanted in the patient's head.

Surgeons in California claim to have produced an electronic ear which is restoring hearing to totally deaf people. The device translates sound vibrations into electricity and then transmits them to the brain.

And yet all these exciting achievements, which not so many years ago would have been scoffed at as sheer fantasy, would probably appear as primitive to a highly-advanced alien society as those blood-sucking leeches and crude surgical instruments of torture from our past appear to us today. And let's face it, how can we yet really justify our medical dexterity when we can't even grow hair on bald heads or outlaw the common cold?

SIX

ARE WE BEING WATCHED?

Never before has man been so aware that someone—
or something—out there could be watching us . . .
perhaps monitoring our technology and way of life,
testing our environment, building up a vast dossier
on our bustling little planet.

Many scientists believe that this extraterrestrial
reconnaissance has been going on for centuries and
that we may just be one of hundreds of other worlds
being individually surveyed by some super-race such
as the Perseans.

How would they have set about such an enormous
task? How could any civilization—including our own—
closely scrutinize so many alien planets millions upon
millions of miles away?

Basically, it can be done in one of two ways. You
can first set up a beacon to attract their attention, followed by direct communication in the form of radio
or laser signals. Or you can send satellites into their

orbits, programmed to automatically carry out their own surveys, exchange information with any intelligence that might make contact, and report back to home base. In this chapter we shall consider both of these systems.

An advanced society would have little difficulty with direct signaling. They would be capable of harnessing vast amounts of solar energy to beam powerful signals deep into space—especially one with an overactive sun such as Gamma Persei.

Man's earliest "beacon" ideas for catching an alien's eye varied from—an enormous mirror to flash reflected sunlight at Mars, massive ditches filled with blazing oil in the Sahara desert to ten-mile-wide strips of trees to form a 280-mile-deep triangle in the Siberian forest. All delightfully illogical, of course.

A more realistic method by a society a little more advanced than ours would be to change the spectrum of its sun. To do this they might infuse a massive quantity of artificial radioactive element into it, thereby producing an "unnatural" spectrum line which would immediately be recognized as such by astronomers on other worlds.

Another method, suggested by Anthony Lawton, is to use an infrared laser beam to change the spectrum of a star by creating in it a narrow band which could be pulsated in sequences so that it would, similarly, be spotted by other planets as artificially induced.

High-powered laser beams might be used to send lengthy messages over a brief transmission period. Millions of items of information could be transmitted in rapidly modulated beams in only a fraction of a second—an achievement that would take many years by radio.

Ordinary light, which rapidly spreads out and is dispersed, would be useless as a signal over any great range. In a laser beam the individual light rays remain parallel to form a narrow, sharply defined beam that can retain its tremendous intensity over long distances.

89

As far back as 1962 a team of scientists at Massachusetts Institute of Technology, using the beam of a ruby laser, were able to illuminate a twenty-mile-wide section of the moon's surface. Equipment was able to detect the beam when it was reflected back to Earth. Had normal light been used, the beam would have fanned out to several times the moon's diameter.

It has been estimated that if a laser beam was passed through the optical system of a giant telescope, such as the one on Mount Palomar, and a similar telescope was operating at the receiving end, a beam could be visible ten light-years away.

Although this is still far short of the penetration of radio waves—hundreds of light-years—laser techniques are still only in their infancy on Earth. Other civilizations may have achieved a stage of laser development that renders radio obsolete.

Lasers offer many advantages. They operate in uncluttered frequency bands not as yet in use. They could also be used to transmit live TV coverage of space probes, such as a manned landing on Mars. And laser contact between spacecraft would require smaller antennae for picking up signals.

But, of course, with all known methods of direct signaling, person-to-person communication would be out of the question with all but the nearest stars, due to the immense transmission delays involved. To send a signal to Gamma Persei, for example, would take 113 years, and a reply would take just as long to come back.

In a paper prepared for the 1973 Russian conference in Baku on communication with extraterrestrial intelligence, Anthony Lawton outlined current ways in which man is trying to achieve this.

The most obvious system within our present economic and technological resources is simply to beam signals by electromagnetic radiation (EMR). Here, as previously explained, twenty-one centimeters seems a logical choice of wavelength to use as it is the wavelength of hydrogen, which is common throughout the universe. Dr. Frank Drake while at the National Radio Astronomy Observatory at Green Bank, West Virginia, used this wavelength to listen for alien signals during Project Ozma in 1960 and '61. Ozma examined two stars approximately ten light-years away—Tau Ceti and Epsilon Eridani—but did not receive signals.

Russia is now listening for possible alien signals in the three-centimeters to fifty-centimeters frequencies over a range of a hundred stars. America recently published a comprehensive design study for a system capable of detecting microwave EMR from extraterrestrial life, called Cyclops (after the legendary one-eyed giant). The following specifications have now been proposed:

1. An installation with a total collecting area initially of seven square kilometers, rising to twenty square kilometers at later phases of research.

2. The area to contain a network of twenty-five hundred electrically phased hundred-meter dish-shaped receiving antennae.

3. The site to be placed in a well-shielded area (ideally in some form of natural bowl) to minimize the effects of man-made interference.

4. The cost, based on 1971 figures, is estimated to average six hundred million dollars per year over a period of thirty years—a total of nearly twenty billion dollars. This covers installation only, and does not include such things as roads and utilities or annual operating labor costs.

This inquisitive monster would be capable of detecting signals over something like twenty thousand light-years. It could also be used for monitoring high-powered stray signals from alien planets. For instance, radio and television signals could be detected at distances up to ten light-years, and radar signals up to twenty-five light-years.

But it is doubtful if any one nation could at present really afford such a costly setup. There would also be a number of disadvantages such as man-made inter-

terence, and natural problems like earthquakes, hurri
canes, and phenomena in the ionosphere. In addition,
installations would be needed in both the northern and
southern hemispheres to fully cover the sky. To be
really worthwhile, systems such as Cyclops would need
to be based on the moon or deep in space, which, of
course, would considerably increase the cost.

Even our presently available equipment could transmit to and receive radio signals from distances up to
a hundred light-years. Installations on the moon,
unimpaired by our atmosphere, could boost this range
to several thousand light-years. This would be useful
in searching for simple identification signals—or
extraterrestrial "call-signs"—but, of course, would
serve little purpose for any manageable two-way
communication over such vast distances.

So, assuming that we already have powerful enough
equipment to send and receive messages with the
nearer stars—those with whom transmission delays
might be confined to a few years—the following conditions would still be necessary for any meaningful
exchange of information:

1. The alien's intelligence must be based on some
form of ordered logic (though this may differ greatly
from our own).

2. They must share with us a common "sense"—
probably vision, which accounts for some eighty percent of the information input to the human brain.

3. The stage of their technology should be not too
widely separated from ours, otherwise one could not
possibly comprehend the other.

4. A common language, or coding system, must be
adapted.

Scientists in various parts of the world are already
studying possible systems. One that could overcome
the language barrier would be to transmit signals that
when correctly decoded produce an actual picture outline or information symbol. And an ingenious form of
this was devised in 1961 by Dr. Drake at Green Bank.

Drake, in fact, proved the ease with which the system could be decoded by trying it out on fellow scientists attending a conference at the observatory. He prepared a sequence of dots and dashes—similar to those used in Morse signaling. The dots would be signified by short radio pulses, and the dashes by longer ones. Most of the scientists were able to decipher the message he gave them.

Received as a continual stream of signals, the dots and dashes would be meaningless. But once these were arranged in a certain scanning pattern—similar to that of a television image—the dots would form an identifiable picture. It's a bit like those pictures we used to make as kids by joining up dots with a pencil. (See Figure 1).

Once a system such as this was mutually accepted, more complex variations of it could enable vast amounts of information to be exchanged. At the

Figure 1

A simple type of digital picture suggested by Drake as an effective means of communicating with extraterrestrials.

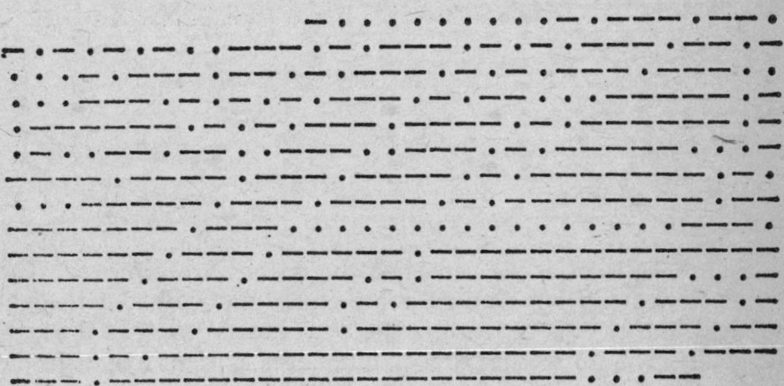

1 a

Figure 1a shows a stream of 450 meaningless dots and dashes (the signal for a dash would last twice as long as that for a dot).

Figure 1b shows the same series of pulses arranged in the correct scanning pattern—with the horizontal rows containing twice those of the verticals—ie. 30 x 15.

1 c

Figure 1c is what we get when the dashes are removed. The large circle (top left) might represent a sun with the straight vertical line of dots beneath it, the five planets (such as those of Perseus). The horizontal row of three dots at right angles to the third planet could be the arms of a very squat, four-legged creature which comes from that planet. The tall figure (center) could be pointing to *his* planet (No. 1). And the spaceship shape (right) might indicate he can travel in his solar system. The curved line of dots, extreme left, could show that he is able to journey from his own planet to planet No. 5.

pulse rate of one per second, 3,600 pieces of information could be transmitted in an hour, 86,400 in a day, or more than 31 million in a year. A simple digital picture like Drake's could be sent in less than ten minutes and could be repeated after short breaks so that any errors or pulses lost by interference could be sorted out.

Though transmitting at one pulse per second is a slow rate, it would enable the receiver to filter out a lot more background noise, and permit good reception of faint signals. And if the message was taped it could, of course, be played back at a much higher speed into a cathode ray "display system," which would "paint" the digital picture line by line.

The correct phasing of each line of signals would be achieved by a special synchronizing system. The results would then be photographed with a camera capable of integrating the line-by-line buildup into a complete picture, such as the one of a spaceman shown in Figure 2.

A good comparison to this kind of digital picture can be found in the way the stitches of a tapestry are made up. Consider the famous Bayeaux tapestry, for instance, which is approximately eighteen inches wide and 226 feet long. If the dimension of each stitch (or piece of information in the picture) is 0.1 inch square, the total number of pieces would be 2.7 x 10^6, or just over two and a half million, which means that the entire historical detail of that tapestry could be transmitted as an interstellar picture in a little over a month at the rate of one pulse per second.

But there are not merely technical problems involved in direct communication with extraterrestrials. There are ethical ones too. For example, should the nation that first makes contact issue an immediate press release so that the world's entire radio-astronomy resources could join forces in organizing the most efficient transmission and receiving techniques? Should it involve a global conference of heads of government

Figure 2

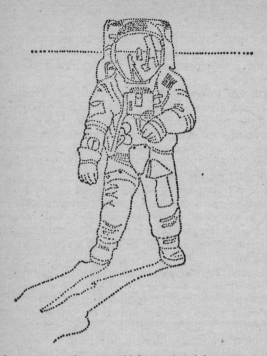

This spaceman picture could be produced by programming 59,200 bits of information in 296 lines of 200 bits per line. At a pulse rate of 1 per second, it could be transmitted in about 16½ hours.

to agree on the type of response man should first make? Or could this result in panic among the less emotionally stable nations?

Before any two-way space talk takes place, should the world's top psychiatrists and sociologists join the astronomers, astrophysicists, and biologists to assess the significance of any alien message? The sequence and manner in which the initial information came to us might well give some insight into the character and motivation of the intelligence that sent it. Before making a reply we could, from analysis of the signals, calculate the distance of the planetary source—and even identify the actual parent star.

If this was, say, five hundred light-years away, we might decide simply to listen in for some years before attempting a reply, since this would not be received by the planet's existing generation and therefore could not result in person-to-person exchanges. Long-term communication such as this could only be acceptable between civilizations with an extremely high degree of social stability—not one such as our own, where international cooperation can fluctuate so dramatically even over short periods of our history. Although, of course, any possible outside threat might unite the human race for the first time.

If the signaling planet were much closer, say within forty light-years, it would be tempting to reply almost immediately, if we recognized their code system. In any case, it would probably be futile to ignore it, as we have already announced our existence to aliens as close as that through stray signals from the normal stream of radioactivity over the years.

A more cautious approach would be to simply listen over a long period to learn as much as we could about an alien, only responding if the messages indicated benign, rather than aggressive, characteristics.

Paradoxically, therefore, the nearest stars—though most suitable for true two-way conversation—could also know our weaknesses and vulnerability. Certainly, those first intelligent signals from outer space are going to test man's diplomacy even more than his technology.

We shall now consider the alternative method of alien contact—through a fully automated satellite. For this is the method most likely to be used by an intelligence as far away as Gamma Persei.

There seems no doubt that before any extraterrestrial intelligence even considered visiting Earth they would first get to know something about us.

If you lived in New York and heard you might have a long-lost cousin in Los Angeles, you wouldn't just go haring off across the country on the slim chance that you might bump into him somewhere. The obvious thing to do would be to check if he had a telephone, find his number from the directory, and put in a call to say you were on your way. If you were pretty sure he couldn't even *use* a phone, let alone possess one, you'd probably forget the whole thing.

An alien intelligence would use similar logic. They might well have been searching their "interstellar directory" of wavelengths for centuries, trying to get a call through to us. And they may have gotten the no reply tone so many times that they gave up trying. We've therefore got to let them know we're now on the universal subscribers' list. That we're on the phone, and can now take long-distance calls.

Now, suppose you later discovered that your long-lost cousin had since gotten himself a phone, learned how to use it, but just wasn't answering. You'd probably ask a local operator to keep the call in—to keep on trying and let you know when she got through. This is precisely what an alien civilization, such as that of Perseus, might be doing right now. But instead of using a local operator they'd be keeping the call in by means of a computerized "brain" contained in an unmanned artifact which they would have placed in orbit around Earth—a space probe such as the one Anthony Lawton and his team are at present trying to locate in their radio experiments in England.

If they *do* find one, it will likely have been monitoring our progress for many years and transmitting its findings back to its home planet.

Centuries ago such probes from Perseus 1 might have started to sweep across the glittering catherine wheel of the Milky Way with its 130,000 million stars and hosts of planets, painstakingly absorbing masses of interstellar information and statistics to feed back to its hungry computers year after year.

Our own solar system would certainly have warranted deeper analysis. Back in the laboratories the Persean computers would have earmarked it as a plausible area for maintaining life. The sun is about right. Not a giant that will rapidly burn itself out or explode into the terrifying fury of a supernova inferno. Not so small as to deprive some of its planetary companions of the warmth and succor from which life must feed. And its age—five thousand million years— would give its planets a reasonable remaining life expectancy.

They would, in fact, have done a very sound reconnaissance job on us.

This is an obvious method of approach. We've been using it ourselves in some form throughout our history. Any experienced army field commander will agree that time spent on reconnaissance is never wasted. So, to help give a clearer picture of just what an alien satellite probe would involve, let's first consider how reconnaissance has developed in our world over the centuries.

Back in the earliest days, hawk-eyed lookouts were vigorously shinning up tall trees or rushing up mountains to increase their visible horizons (remote reconnaissance). Or they were gingerly infiltrating well-disguised spies with very good memories into enemy camps, hoping they'd get out again with a few vital scraps of information (close reconnaissance). The Bible gives us examples of both these methods. Moses climbed Mount Nebo, four thousand feet above sea level (Deuteronomy, Chapter 34), and could see as far as the Western Sea (Mediterranean) and Northern Galilee—which meant he had a view of nearly a hundred miles, which even gave him a remote glimpse of Israel.

Chapter 2 of Joshua quotes a good example of

close reconnaissance which two men are sent secretly to Jericho to spy on the city's fortifications. The information paid off handsomely for the Israelites. Jericho fell.

These two methods of reconnaissance remained virtually unchanged until World War I. Aircraft were introduced, and very soon aerial photography was born, making it possible to scan wider areas for vast stores of information about the enemy. Here, literally, was the spy in the camp, able to remain there and transmit his news by radio.

These techniques rapidly developed in World War II. In 1943 the Allies were even able to photograph the German V-1 flying bomb, from forty thousand feet, as a tiny airplane-type image on a railway track. And later that year, agents on the ground were so well organized that they smuggled a complete flying bomb out of enemy territory and into Allied hands.

The year 1957 saw the launching of the Russian Sputnik 1 and satellite photography began in earnest. Now, in 1973, the world's major powers have sentinel satellites—sophisticated peeping Toms which can tell each of them what the other side is up to.

Very little eludes these searching guardian angels of the sky. The setting up of a space rocket can be monitored from the moment the vehicle is trundled onto the site to the launch countdown. And there are many ways in which satellites are helping to keep tabs on environmental changes and seek out vital mineral deposits, spotting forest fires and surveying possible new areas for crop growing. We can now use infrared photography and television techniques which use heat instead of visible light.

In the 1973 Middle East conflict, the "spy" satellites of the leading world powers were capable of not only counting the numbers of tanks and aircraft used by either side but of also identifying the types.

But, although our aerial "spy" network has developed enormously in less than sixty years, we cannot as yet keep a satellite in a close, stable orbit around Earth for very long periods. This is because the moon, circling Earth, would disturb a satellite until it eventually spiraled out of orbit into the atmosphere and burned up.

So to be able to carry out greatly extended surveys we would need to do either of two things. We could land the "spy" on the moon and scan our world as the moon revolved around it. Or we could place the "spy" in an orbit which the moon could *not* disturb.

As it happens, such orbits do exist. They are called *Lagrange*, or *Trojan*, orbits. These orbits are the same distance from Earth as the moon—around 240,000 miles—and once a satellite got into one of these areas, the gravitational pull of Earth and moon would be more evenly balanced. It would, therefore, be a very long time before it drifted out.

Now, let's assume an alien "spy" satellite or probe, such as one from Perseus, wishes to set itself up in one of these orbits so that it can monitor Earth for signs of life and, more important, evidence of a growing technology. How would it set about this complicated project?

The navigation of such a probe would be achieved in several stages. First, the computers aboard would be programmed to slow it down to, say, twenty percent of the speed of light as it approached to within half a light-year of our sun. The computers could then make an accurate account of the positions of the various stars about them. Ahead of the probe would be the sun—easily the brightest object in view. The probe would then automatically head toward it, slowing down even more as it did so.

The next maneuvers would depend largely on the angle of the course on which the probe was approaching the sun, but it would probably look for what is known as the Zodiacal Light—stray sunlight scattered from the dust and debris surrounding the sun. All the planets lie in this blanket of dust, and the probe, while still keeping the sun in its sights, would correct its course until it lay in the plane of the Zodiacal Light.

It would then slow down even more, and move around the sun in a sweeping path, similar to that taken by a comet. Now traveling at only about one percent of the speed of light, it would have plenty of time to look around.

As soon as the sun's radiance and heat reached the correct level of intensity—which would be the temperature at which ice melts—it would change its orbit to become a fixed part of the solar system . . . in fact, a satellite of the sun. From this position it would look for bright bodies other than the sun—namely, the orbiting planets. It would see Mercury as merely a pinpoint of light. Mars and Venus would be large enough discs to be examined.

An alien satellite might wish to do a grand tour of our entire solar system, though this is unlikely due to the wastage of fuel. If it did, however, its restless probe would move from planet to planet as its computers sifted, tabulated, and analyzed the territorial makeup and conditions of each. It would find Pluto—the small outcast of the solar family—cold, lonely, forbidding, devoid of friendly atmosphere, silent, and utterly desolate with lifeless deserts frozen motionless around the stark deformity of rock. A computer would register a rating of nil for a galactic dungeon such as this.

Next it would find the great blue barrenness of Neptune, nearly three thousand miles from the glow of the sun, still frozen solid in temperatures of −350° F., with its equally uninviting satellites, Triton and Nereid, in funereal attendance. Again—a negative grading.

On to Uranus—another giant by Earthly standards, with its 29,300-mile diameter and five small satellites. But here again there is little in the planet's cold solitude to attract our solar-searching race.

Saturn, the uniquely glorious spectacle ringed by myriads of ice-coated meteoritelike particles, would also be given a negative grading, in spite of its beauty. The probe would still find little encouragement for life. Saturn is intensely cold and has a gaseous surface which rules out any actual landing attempts by space travelers.

From the deceiving beauty of Saturn, the probe would move on to the largest of the sun's wards— Jupiter. Like our own *Pioneer 10*, the alien probe would savor its turbulence, and register the violence of its storms, which can burst with as much angry energy in a fleeting second as is generated by a hundred thousand million Earthly strokes of lightning.

It might even detect evidence of some life form on this mighty gaseous body—perhaps balloonlike creatures sucking in hydrogen instead of oxygen and feeding on the ammonia of their foreboding environment. But, as *Pioneer 10* has discovered, the probe would realize that this was no place for strangers.

On through the swarms of asteroids—those thousands of swirling bits of heavenly debri that separate Jupiter from its next neighbor, Mars. Here the computers would face the tantalizing problem that Earthmen have argued over for centuries: Could *this* be a life supporter? It has an atmosphere of sorts—though extremely tenuous and practically devoid of oxygen. Its rugged, crater-ravaged deserts of red dust and rock, and its extreme temperatures, would not make it a particularly cozy planet to live on, but with a little improvisation, life there would not seem impossible.

Therefore, a probe might list it among the possibles. Only when the satellite's sensors moved in on Earth would the Martian territory drop out of the running. Here, full positive readings would be registered for abundant oxygen and water. Here would be the cosmic El Dorado it had journeyed so far to find.

The probe would therefore start to change its orbit. From being a satellite of the sun, it would become a satellite of Earth. Here, the computers would have to clear up one final problem. Their target planet, Earth, would already have a satellite—and a big one . . . the moon. Delving into its program once more, it would decide to move into the Trojan orbit of Earth, which we referred to earlier in this chapter.

So, let's just summarize the probe's complete schedule of maneuvers from the moment it approaches our system, by quoting the following instructions from its computer brain:

1. Slow down to ten percent of the speed of light. We're nearly there. Now look for the sun and move toward it.

2. Find the Zodiacal Light and maneuver into the dust blanket around the sun while still heading for the sun.

3. Approach it to within a distance that corresponds to the melting point of water, and move into its orbit.

4. Seek out the planets while cruising around the sun, and scan each planet for water and oxygen.

5. Select the planet that has both, and move into its orbit to become one of its satellites.

6. To allow for the moon's gravity pull, settle down finally in a Trojan orbit around Earth.

7. Activate sensors to infeed data for any signs of intelligent life, and collate the information.

8. Record bright-star coordinates (brightness and position) to inform any intelligence on the target planet of probe's location and purpose.

9. Process the star-position coordinates and relate them to Gamma Persei so that the correct identification signals can be produced in subsequent information exchanges, should they take place.

10. Start routine signals to attract attention.

From the time of the brain's initial slow-down instruction to the moment those vital life-seeking sensors are switched on and photography and signaling has started, those ten maneuvers would have taken three months to one year to complete.

There can be no short-cut for this gigantic project. The planets must be accurately identified against a star-studded background before the final search for life can be made. And slow, methodical operations are not only more accurate, they also involve less mechanical stress on the probe satellite's structure. In any case, for an alien society that may have to wait perhaps from two hundred to six hundred years for its first news flashes, a few months' preparation is neither here nor there. Surely it is far wiser to exercise care to ensure an endamaged, workable probe than to sabotage the whole project by reckless impatience.

An alien "brain" may well be now circling Earth from stars such as Perseus in precisely the way as has been described—safe in the shelter of a Trojan orbit and unobtrusively observing us for signs of civilized life, patiently waiting for an opportunity to establish communication with us. How it might do this, and how its signals might be recognized by our scientsts, is described in Chapter 7.

Let us now consider what sort of things an alien satellite could be noting about us and what conclusions it might be drawing. Remember, as we said earlier, "time spent in reconnaissance is never wasted." And consider the rapid advances our own survey satellites have made in the short time we have had them. Imagine the technical wizardry of a probe created by a super-race.

One of its first concerns would be to look for clues to our stage of technological and sociological development. They would assess the amount of energy we were using, as the more advanced a civilization is, the more energy it burns up; a technology-oriented society uses a lot of energy.

In poverty-stricken, underdeveloped countries dried cow dung is still used as fuel for cooking. On the other hand, the average Western housewife, with her deep freezer, food mixer, cooker, dish-warmer, dish washer, and all the rest of her electrical cooking aids, uses enough energy on one meal to keep an Eastern family living (in the manner to which they are accustomed) for a month.

This does not take into account the energy used up to produce the electricity in the first place, nor the energy which melted the metals and cooked the plastics needed to make all that kitchen paraphernalia and all those food containers.

Technological civilizations like ours are using energy at an enormous rate and, as the underdeveloped countries start to catch up, they too will be making equally overwhelming demands.

As this takes place, something quite significant will happen to Earth. It will become slightly warmer—enough to actually be shown in the amount of heat radiated from our planet. An alien probe, registering this steady rise of heat, would be able to assess the rate at which we were using energy—and, hence, the level of our technology. True, there can be natural reasons for changes in our heat output—variations in cloud reflection, alternations in the radiation from the sun—but a probe such as the one we are considering could easily distinguish these.

Another obvious clue to our technology would be the amount of carbon dioxide in our atmosphere. This steadily increases as we burn oil, coal, and gas. This loss is not replaced by our plant life (which normally takes in carbon dioxide and uses it to produce oxygen and foodstuffs) because we are frantically scooping up acres of land for houses, factories, and roads, and plants don't generally grow in these areas. So up and away goes the carbon dioxide and, as the probe would probably be equipped with a spectrometer, it would accurately measure this increase.

The probe might have occasionally measured tremendous, but very short, electrical pulses (called EMP), together with high-temperature flashes. The "brain" would register: "Planet has attained knowledge of explosive release of nuclear power."

But the greatest clue to any civilization must be its widespread use of radio waves for communications. Whatever more-sophisticated methods they may eventually develop, all cultures must go through the phase of using radio systems to communicate. And, brother, do we communicate!

Powerful radio stations throughout the world are belting out the voices of nations at several kilowatts, and thousands of smaller stations are contributing their own few hundred watts. There are millions of radio-controlled taxis, aircraft, boats, and trains. Worldwide transmitters pump out hundreds of kilowatts of "picture power" for our television sets.

And, finally, we come to the really big stuff—radar defense systems, early-warning and ballistic-missile stations, and the rest. And these don't just operate in kilowatts, but in megawatts (a kilowatt is a thousand watts, a megawatt is a million watts).

As all this global chatter goes on, we must be easily overheard by any orbiting space probe. And we're not only announcing ourself to a computer brain; if a civilization exists in our nearest star system—Alpha Centauri, 4.3 light-years away—they too could know about us. Because, if we take a typical radar system with a "dish," or antenna, about 120 feet across, and belt one megawatt of power into it, any inquisitive aliens with a similar dish and a good receiver could hear us even from twelve light-years away. True, the signals would take twelve years to get there, but they would receive them all right. And there are at least six sunlike stars within that distance.

But the puny power of a 120-foot dish pales into insignificance when we compare it to the mighty roar of the Arecibo dish in Puerto Rico when its radar research bounces signals off other planets. And an even more thunderous roar will emerge from the giant

Russian dish at Ratan when it, too, starts radar sounding.

Signals from these devices could be picked up over hundreds of light-years if our alien cousins had similar antennae, and within a radius of only a hundred light-years are more than a thousand stars exactly like our own sun. If we double this range the number rises to more than ten thousand stars, which almost certainly have planets, some of which may well sustain intelligent life. It is almost almost certain that other inhabited planets will hear signals from such installations.

Both of the dishes at Arecibo and Ratan have now been fitted with supersensitive radio receivers which, coupled with their mighty transmitters, would allow us to "speak" right across our galaxy—a matter of a hundred sixty thousand light-years. Aliens with similar listening devices may, at this very moment, be eavesdropping on our radio chatter.

Our first signals of any real power went out in the early 1920s, which means we could have already announced ourselves to civilizations up to fifty light-years away—or in the vicinity of about a hundred sunlike stars.

Radio signaling is the one positive hallmark of any technological civilization—the signature of an advancing culture written clearly in the universe. The following well-quoted lines of Omar Khayam could not be more applicable: "The moving finger writes—and having writ, moves on. Nor all thy toil nor all thy tears shall wash away one word of it."

For radio signals travel on and on into space, and even though they get fainter and fainter, there must be many astute listeners out there who will have the means to recognize them—even when submerged in the natural noise of the galaxy.

None of this is science fiction. It is science fact. The Project Cyclops blueprint from Stanford University was specifically designed to listen for signals from other stars. To quote from page 59 of the official report: "We conclude that if we keep on broadcasting our TV signals for another century, Earth will be 'visible' up to something on the order of a hundred light-years, which could announce our existence to beings on any of the thousand or more likely star systems within that range. To beings that detected us, there would not be doubt for very long that the signal was the work of Man, not Nature." And these are the cold, measured words of a NASA report prepared by top men in the United States.

It is precisely this kind of unmistakable evidence an alien probe orbiting Earth would be programmed to watch out for and respond appropriately to. These responses may have already been made, but not yet been recognized by mankind. Only by specifically directing radio signals at the Lagrange or Trojan areas (areas where Earth orbits can be maintained without disturbance from the moon) will we know for certain whether or not a probe really does exist.

Trojan areas are being photographed by *Skylab*. Will a peculiar object—one that is neither natural nor *man*-made—be visible? If an alien probe *is* there, could we spot it among the countless dots and specks that will represent stars, micrometeorites, planetoids, photographic plate flaws, and dust?

If a probe *is* located and *is* alerted by radio signals, we will go out there and inspect it carefully. The first step, after long-distance photography, would be to move in closer with a reconnaissance satellite to obtain more photographs and television images for transmission back to Earth. We would approach the object with extreme caution. It may well be programmed to destroy intruders.

If this remote check-up reports it safe to handle, larger space laboratories could move in, followed, finally, by a manned Apollo or Soyuz craft to thoroughly inspect it.

Imagine the scientific fascination of studying such an object—a mechanical intelligence capable of near-

109

human, two-way conversation, able to transmit data back to its creators, perhaps two-hundred light years away. A machine that has been powered and navigated over such incredible distances and survived after finding its own way to Earth.

And most intriguing of all—though it may be unique in our solar system, hundreds more of its kind could be carrying out the same search for life in other parts of our galaxy, perhaps many of them launched by one super-race . . . and that race could come from a planet of the actual star system of Perseus—a system which scientists accept as being quite likely to have life-supporting planets.

What would be the cost of sending our own such satellites to other solar systems if we were equipped with interstellar rockets? The Cyclops team figured the cost of a million probes needed to cover all likely stars within a thousand light-years of the sun as 10^{13} (ten trillion) dollars, and that at the rate of one probe per day it would take a total of three thousand years to launch them! Bracewell, however, has speculated that a thousand stars within a hundred light-years could be explored by space probes. And a thousand probes could be launched in thirty years, at a cost comparable to that of building a Cyclops complex on Earth. As mentioned earlier, the Perseans would have had to launch up to five hundred probes to be sure of finding suitable new worlds.

Bracewell, in recent articles and correspondence, still maintains his belief that the best means of conveying large amounts of data over very large distances (greater than a hundred light-years) is by computerized satellites, simply because they could produce a noise-free signal at any suitable frequency.

They could also offer a practical form of two-way communication with the probe's brain, exchanging information within seconds instead of the many years needed by any direct planet-to-planet contact. Even a modest sixty-watt transmitter based on the moon will produce an adequate signal in an aerial dish of less than twenty meters—compared with 2.5 megawatts used by a Cyclops complex for direct communication with a star system only twenty light-years away.

But whatever methods man uses, he must go on searching. And if he receives a signal which can *only* be interpreted as "We live on one of the planets of an Orange Giant star"—it will be one of the most tragic events in astronomical history. For our first awakening to interstellar communication would be through the death cry of a doomed civilization—one such as Perseus 1—whose sun had begun to incinerate it.

SEVEN

ECHOES FROM OUTER SPACE

If the kind of alien satellite discussed in the previous chapter actually *is* out there orbiting Earth, how would its delicately programmed computer brain be attempting to attract our attention? How would we know, and what possible common language could there be between humans and some other intelligence from space? Have alien signals, in fact, actually been received without us recognizing them as such?

To consider this dramatic possibility we shall further analyze the sensational announcement in 1973 by Scottish astronomer Duncan Lunan when he claimed to have interpreted long-delayed signals—or echoes of signals—he believes originated from an extraterrestrial probe. We shall also present the views, and the alternative speculatiton, of Anthony Lawton, the man actively engaged in checking out this possibility.

Sections of this chapter must, therefore, be some-what technical. But to assist the lay reader, it is pre-

sented in as direct a form as possible without losing what will be essential detail to the more scientifically minded reader. Lunan translated these echoes to read:

"He translates the message:

" 'Start here. Our home is Upsilon Bootis, which is a double star. We live on the sixth planet of seven. Check that—the sixth of seven counting outwards from the sun, which is the larger of the two.

" 'Our sixth planet has one moon. Our fourth planet has three. Our first and third planets each have one.

" 'Our probe is in the position of Arcturus, known in our maps.'

Lunan claims he has been able to arrange a sequence of fourteen mysterious echoes of varying delay times into a map, or chart, of the star constellation Epsilon Boötes. The echoes were reported in Europe in 1928 and '29 by two professors, Van der Pol and Carl Störmer, while listening in to signals from radio station PCJJ.

How did Lunan do this? If you study the graph in Figure 3 you will see that the base line shows a series of echo-delay times from zero to fifteen seconds to cover the variable range of the Van der Pol sequence, which was 8,11,15,8,13,3,8,8,8,12,15,13,8,8, seconds. The upright line shows the order in which echoes were apparently received and recorded. A dot is then marked on the graph at the point where the delay time and the sequence number of each echo coincides.

You will see that the eight-second dots form a straight row—or "barrier." On the left there is a single dot (or "lone star") corresponding to a three-second echo delay. On the right the dots form an incomplete map of the constellation which Lunan interprets as Boötes.

Figure 3   The first Van der Pol Sequence
October 11, 1928

This is graphed exactly as recorded by Van der Pol

Pulse Sequence No.	1	2	3	4	5	6	7	8	9	10	11	12	13	14
Echo Delay Time in seconds	8	11	15	8	13	3	8	8	8	12	15	13	8	8

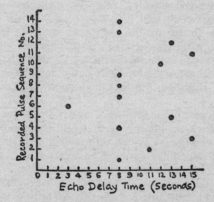

This is a precisely graphed star map using the sequence of
echoes received by Van der Pol on the night of October 11,
1928. The delay times of the echoes, in seconds, are shown
along the horizontal base line of the graph and their sequence
number along the vertical line. By intersecting these, we get the
formation of dots as shown.

By regarding the eight-second dots as a "barrier," Lunan
claims that the sequence produces an incomplete map of the

star constellation Boötes (the Herdsman). By moving the three-second echo dot across to the other side of the barrier, the constellation, he says, is completed.

However, Anthony Lawton has now been able to obtain the records of further sequences received in November 1928 and February 1929, and they do not bear any resemblance to constellations. Lawton believes that long-delayed echoes are more common than was first thought.

One star is missing from the known system. This, Lunan argues, is deliberately left out of the "message" from the probe to indicate that it is, in fact, the key star—or the star of the civilization that launched the probe in the first place.

This form of message, he says, demands an intelligent reply. To make it, we transmit this same star map back to the orbiting probe (by sending the same sequence of delayed signals). *But*—we make one vital alteration. We switch that lone dot (star) on the left of the graph across to the right—to a spot which corresponds to a thirteen-second delay. This then completes the star constellation Boötes and also lets the probe know that we are sufficiently intelligent to transcribe its message. Further communication could then begin.

Not only does Lunan use the Van der Pol sequence of echoes to back up his theory, but also some experiments made in May 1929 by a three-day French expedition to Indochina (now Vietnam) which was making observations during an eclipse of the sun. They too reported delayed echoes with their five-hundred-watt shortwave transmitter. Although Lunan does not produce a map or chart of the Boötes constellation from these echoes, he claims they form other star systems.

Is Lunan's interpretation acceptable? Were those 1928–29 long-delayed radio echoes really from an alien artifact, or were they caused by some natural phenomena?

116

In a serious attempt to answer this, part of Anthony Lawton's research in the summer of 1973 compared some 1928 echoes with other more recent LDE (long-delayed echoes) reports whose eminent observers believe *do* have a natural origin.

To do this, Lawton has now actually traced the man who assisted Sir Edward Appleton of King's College, London. Appleton—like Van der Pol and Störmer—was receiving long-delayed echoes from radio station PCJJ transmissions in Holland in 1928 and '29. Appleton's assistant, R.L.A. Borrow, clearly recalls receiving these echoes.

Lawton then carefully checked them against LDEs reported in 1970 by Professor F.W. Crawford of Stanford University and by Professor O.G. Villard of Stanford Research Institute who has published precisely collated results of some ninety-two LDE reports from amateur radio operators from 1968 to '71. Lawton now confirms that "the LDEs received from PCJJ by Appleton and Borrow at King's College do, indeed, bear a strong resemblance to the phenomena reported by Villard and Crawford." And Crawford says he believes the ones *he* received were caused by signal reflection and amplification due to certain natural conditions within the upper ionosphere.

It is also possible, claims Lawton, that—despite certain variations in the Van der Pol–Störmer echoes from which Duncan Lunan compiled his star map of Epsilon Boötis—"slightly different natural phenomena mechanisms were responsible for these too."

Crawford believes that his long-delayed echoes were caused by what are termed *plasma interactions* in the ionosphere. This means that when a radio wave traveling—as light does—at 186,000 miles per second enters plasma (or gas cloud), its speed is reduced to only half a mile per second as long as it remains there. Once it leaves the cloud again, it accelerates back to the speed of light.

117

Lawton can now confidently account for those varying delays in the Van der Pol series of 1928 echoes by taking Crawford's theory further. The short, undistorted echoes from one to five seconds would result from radio waves entering small, stationary or slow-moving clouds. The long, distorted ones (five to thirty seconds or more) would be caused by larger clouds whose shapes rapidly vary, like the turbulent clouds of a thunderstorm. Under certain conditions these clouds act as big radio amplifiers. (A more detailed explanation of this process is contained in Appendix 3.)

In a letter to Lawton, Borrow (Appleton's assistant) recalls PCJJ listening tests he carried out each morning between six and eight A.M. and also in the afternoon, from October 1928 to June 1929. The letter X, in Morse, was transmitted every thirty seconds, leaving time to receive any echoes up to that length of delay. (An exact sequence is given in Appendix 3.) On at least one occasion he obtained a perfect record of the initial transmission and the echo, and he goes on:

"During the trials, which involved over 150 hours of listening, I heard very few echoes—not more than ten. The echoes arrived at random times and I do not recollect ever hearing more than one echo from any emission [as Van der Pol had done]. I am very suspicious of many of the claims I have heard where the observer has stated that he has frequently heard echoes of long delay. I have spent a lot of time listening to transmissions of various types on a multitude of frequencies and I have *never* heard an echo which I would describe as of long delay from any transmission except those from the Hague." (PCJJ.)

Following this letter, Lawton met Borrow and obtained a good description of the quality and type of apparatus used for the reception and photography of the PCJJ transmissions. "We are," writes Lawton, "reasonably assured that the apparatus did receive genuine LDEs and had a high degree of sophistication for those times."

Borrow also clearly remembered the type of echo he received—one direct repeat of the signal, delayed by one to twenty-eight seconds. Lawton points out: "The echoes were extremely rare—only one LDE per thousand test transmissions from PCJJ, a figure which closely agrees with those quoted by Crawford and Villard. Furthermore, these LDEs were distributed at random. There were no apparent sequences, as reported by Störmer and Van der Pol." We have now obtained the actual notes made by Borrow in 1928.

So far Lawton has found that that the Appleton–Borrow LDEs of 1928 and '29, and the recent ones of Villard and Crawford, *conform* in five ways—a conclusion now confirmed by Villard. They are:

1. The echoes were single repeats of the original transmission, being delayed by one to twenty-eight seconds. There were no sequences.

2. On very rare occasion a second consecutive transmission produced a consecutive echo. This second echo was much fainter and any phenomena due to further consecutive transmission were lost in noise.

3. The echoes were rare (average one per thousand transmissions).

4. They were clearly recognizable reproductions of the original transmission and there was no blurring as reported by Van der Pol.

5. The lack of Doppler Shift (the change in frequency caused by objects moving away or toward an observer) was noted in both the Appleton and Villard reports. Crawford too mentions this effect for some of his LDEs.

Based on the above similarities, Lawton concludes: "The LDEs reported by Appleton in 1928–29 were real, and were not due to faulty mechanism or auditory hallucination.

"The cause of these echoes was very similar to (if not identical with) that proposed by Crawford.

119

"These LDEs were *not* due to an alien artifact."

All the evidence, in fact, strongly supports Crawford's theory that they were caused by reflection in the upper ionosphere. And this theory is a modification of the one originally put forward by Van der Pol. (A more detailed explanation of this, together with sketches of the King's College radio receiving system, is contained in Appendix 3.)

Lawton is now testing modified versions of Crawford's theory in his current radio-transmission experiments and hopes to produce similar LDEs at higher frequencies.

He raises other loopholes in Lunan's interpretation, and does not agree that the original Van der Pol echoes—or, at least, the reported sequence of them that we so far possess—makes up a genuine and scientifically acceptable star-constellation map. For instance, we do not know how the sequence was obtained. Was it taken from consecutive echoes or were they distributed at random through the transmissions? Von der Pol only recorded fourteen known echoes from a total of 120 pulses or signals. Did those fourteen echoes all follow consecutive pulses, or were they random?

Lawton now has several reasons to believe that they were not consecutive echoes.

Another flaw in the Boötes map is that it contains too few accurately placed stars to fit the true constellation. Four are missing. Lawton has also researched the records of the 1929 French expedition to Indochina (Vietnam) to observe a solar eclipse and says that the chances of them meaning anything significant range from one in ten to one in forty-five.

The most common LDE times reported over the years are those of three and eight seconds. The former could well be caused by reflection from the surface of the moon. One American researcher, C. R. Clarke, has noted that the frequency of these three-second reports appear to be associated with the moon's

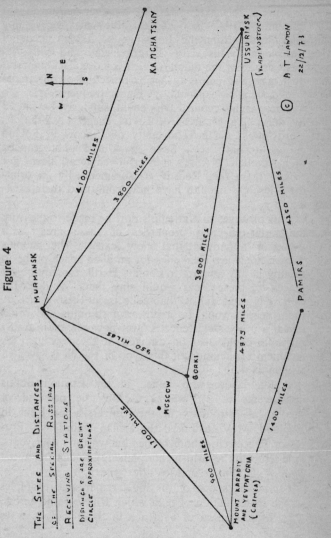

Figure 4

The Sites and Distances
of the Special Russian
Receiving Stations

Distances are Great
Circle Approximations

N
W — E
S

MURMANSK

KAMCHATSKIY

4.100 MILES

3800 MILES

950 MILES

3800 MILES

GORKI

MOSCOW

4875 MILES

4250 MILES

900 MILES

1100 MILES

MOUNT KARADIY
AND YEVPATORIA
(CRIMEA)

1400 MILES

PAMIRS

USSURIYSK
(VLADIVOSTOCK)

© A T LAWTON
22/12/73

121

nonith angle. Lawton, in a paper for the Russian conference on extraterrestrial communication in the autumn of 1973, also suggests they may be coming back to us from the Lagrange or Trojan areas of the moon (areas sixty degrees ahead and sixty degrees astern of the moon) which could collect sufficient dust, gas, and debris to act as reflectors of our transmitted signals—especially at higher frequencies.

Those eight-second LDEs could, similarly, be caused by the Lagrange areas of Earth, suggests Clarke. K. Kordylewski of the University of Cracow in Poland claims to have seen these areas and photographed them though NASA's powerful cameras have not picked them out. Recent measurements by an orbiting telescope satellite have now confirmed their existence.

Lawton urges that attempts now be made to measure the radar-reflecting properties of these areas with powerful apparatus that now exists. The moon's Trojan areas are ideal sites for an alien space probe to occupy in any attempt to contact Earth, for any object placed in these areas would stay there, as does the dust, gas, and debris that collects in these areas. A radar search would be a powerful stimulus and could reveal a probe's existence. Lower-powered radio transmissions could also be directed at these points. (A technical explanation of this type of search is given in Appendix 4.)

Among those who joined in the Epsilon Boötis controversy in 1973 was G. C. McVittie, professor of theoretical astronomy at the University of Kent in England. McVittie raised the Lunan theory with Professor Bracewell, whom he has known for many years. In a letter to the British Interplanetary Society's journal *Spaceflight*, Professor McVittie writes:

"It provides one of the most remarkable examples of the manipulation of data which I have come across. . . . Manipulation of evidence in these various ways does not add up to a scientific procedure and, indeed, would be rejected out of hand in any court of law."

Briefly, these were some examples of "manipulation" listed by McVittie:

1. Lunan only identifies as stars certain points on the diagram he compiled from the Van der Pol sequence of long-delayed echoes.

2. Without any supporting evidence, he asserts that the vertical series of eight-second echo delays are not star positions, but are meant to form a "barrier."

3. Moving the three-second echo-delay point to the thirteen-second spot does not give a true formation of the Boötes constellation. Lunan says it would have appeared like *his* map thirteen thousand years ago, but there is no evidence of this.

4. Other three-second delay echoes were being received by engineer Hals *before* the Van der Pol sequence began. If these had also to be switched across the eight-second barrier, they would have made very little sense of the Epsilon Boötis indentification.

5. There is no evidence to prevent many other maps of star systems, other than Boötis, from being formed by similar manipulation of the available sequence of echo delays.

If the Van der Pol sequence of delayed echoes *had* been deliberately arranged by an alien probe to represent a star map of Boötis, what about those echoes received by Appleton at about the same time? How do *they* fit in with the theory?

Late in 1973 Lawton was able to trace the actual records of the Appleton echoes. He has composed a star map from them. (See Figure 5.) They in no way conform to the Van der Pol sequence. In fact, if one wished to apply the Boötis reasoning (which we don't), the constellation that comes closest to the shape formed by these echoes is Perseus.

It must be emphasized, however, that we are *not* claiming that Appleton's long-delayed echoes, or any others so far recorded, were *intended* to represent

123

Perseus. We selected this particular star system to symbolize the theme of this book because it is one believed suitable for sustaining life. Its inhabitants *could* be trying to contact us, because one of its suns *could* be dying. It just so happens that the star map Lawton has produced from one of Appleton's sequence of echoes (using the same principle Lunan applied to plotting Epsilon Boötis) fits Perseus more closely than any other constellation. (See Figure 5.)

Though his investigations may finally disprove Duncan Lunan's Epsilon Boötis theory, Anthony Lawton believes he may still find evidence for alien messages among the host of amateur reports of LDEs that crop up. His search project has only just begun. His powerful radio equipment may well seek out an orbiting probe waiting for the opportunity to communicate with us.

He is convinced, however, that to produce a genuine map of a star constellation, able to contain sufficient detail for a deliberate message—perhaps even including the location of planets—a sequence of echoes would need to contain not only delays of varying times, but also zeros—or no echoes at all to some of our signals.

These zeros, or spaces, are necessary in order to punctuate the "words" of the message. For instance, if we write IAIMATWHATIAM, that is a sequence of thirteen characters, but is not a clear message. However, if we write I AIM AT WHAT I AM, we have inserted five zeroes, or spaces, in the thirteen characters. This zero-content of nearly forty percent now produces a precise message.

Mathematically, these are called *meaningful zeros*. The principle of using these meaningful zeros—or *nil returns*—is, to some extent, similar to that used by an organization wishing to set up a public-opinion poll. They would never get a balanced result entirely from *yes* and *no* replies. There are always a proportion of neutral voters who reply that they don't know. Both Lawton and Bracewell are convinced that an

Figure 5

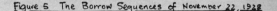

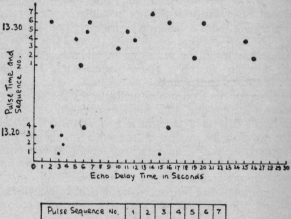

Figure 5 The Borrow Sequences of November 22, 1928

This is a "star map" composed from the long-delayed echoes obtained by R.L.A. Borrow on November 22, 1928. It is obvious they do not bear any accurate resemblance to known star constellations. Borrow's laboratory notes, which we have now traced, are probably the most accurate records ever taken from the transmissions of radio station PCJJ.

acceptable star map would contain a proportion of these zeros. Lunan's star map doesn't.

Lawton has, therefore, produced a number of constellation sketches that make significant use of these important zeros, or nil returns.

He considers that to produce a star map with both sufficient *and* accurate information, the number of zeros needed is about one-third to one-half of the total number of echoes in a sequence. This would allow a probe to give sufficient detail for us to rule out the chances of the echoes being purely random ones. In other words, a star map providing this amount of evidence could not possibly be interpreted as anything but a genuine extraterrestrial form of contact. The chances of it being caused by natural phenomena would be only one in millions. And with such a set of signals a star's planets could be quite clearly shown and plotted.

The graph in Figure 6 actually forms the star constellation of Perseus, and shows five planets . . . those five small dots in a horizontal row at the top. *If* we were to actually receive a sequence of signals that produced such a formation, we would assume that those five dots were planets because there are not star positions in the actual constellation to correspond to those dots. And we would have already established that the principal star placings (the large dots) were accurate.

In transmission as radio signals, those five planet dots would have been fainter than the others.

As you can see, this star map has been made up from seventeen echoes and nine zero returns. If this map *were* received, we could quite simply rule out the possibility of it being any other constellation by matching the echo pattern with other major star formations—checking both from left to right and from an upside down position.

This check would be made by a computer, which would be more than likely to come up with a number of

Figure 6
How a star map of the constellation of Perseus would be formed if the echo delay times shown had been received.

Pulse No.	1	2	3	4	5	6	7	8	9	10	11
Echo Delay	0	0	5	0	0	0	13	5 12	0	7	11

Pulse No.	12	13	14	15	16	17			18	19	20
Echo Delay	0	8	9	10	14	13 14 15 16 17 18			0	14	0

20 Pulses, 26 Echoes — What do they mean?

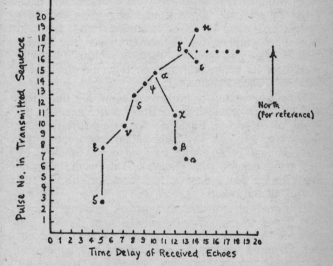

The echoes graphed against the pulse sequence. The graph eventually proved to be a representation of the star constellation "Perseus." But why the Five little echoes after the single large one for transmitted pulse No. 17?
Could it be that ɣ (Gamma) Persei has five planets and that the probe came from one of them?

alternative constellations that matched the pattern. These would then be "screened" to find the star system most likely to be of a type possessing planets and where conditions might be such that intelligent life could have developed on one or more of them.

Let us assume we *have*, in fact, established that the constellation was that of Perseus. How could the inhabitants who sent the probe possibly know what its own arrangement of stars and planets looked like from Earth?

They couldn't know. The computer onboard its probe would have remembered the course it had navigated to get here. Once it had arrived in the solar system and taken up its orbit around Earth, it would have photographed the sky, programmed the images into its brain and projected them as a clear "identikit" picture of its native star system. It would show what Perseus looked like from Earth.

How do we tell a probe we know it's out there and we know where it came from? Refer again to the graph of Perseus in Figure 6. We would first transmit pulse No. 17—the key pulse (that representing the star Gamma Persei) with its loud echo, followed by five small echoes (the planets). This would demonstrate to the probe that we had identified the key star out of all the others.

It would also assure the probe's computer brain that it was in contact with an intelligent receiver and decoder. And remember—that is all we are at present. An advanced civilization would have had equipment for automatically decoding interstellar signals for centuries.

Once we had decoded that first star map, the probe might then send us a second sequence that would produce Figure 7. Here we have only eight dots—five large ones and three small ones. You will notice that the two large dots at the top of the graph are very close together, almost like a dash. This could be intended to show us that Gamma Persei has a binary

Figure 7

Pulse No	1	2	3		4	5	6	94 MORE ZEROS	100	101	102	103	104	105
Echo Delay	0	0	5 6 7 8 10 14		0	0	0		0	0	0	0	0	5·0 5·5

105 Pulses, 8 Echoes — What do these mean?

When graphed against the pulse sequence the echoes give the two parts of Gamma Persei.

The top double echo is one star, itself a binary.

The bottom series gives the main star and its planets.

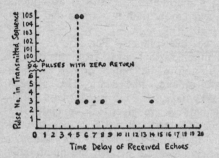

Pulse No. in Transmitted Sequence

94 PULSES WITH ZERO RETURN

Time Delay of Received Echoes

How a further series of delayed echoes from a Persean probe satellite might be transmitted to produce a map of the star and the planets.

star system—that is, two stars or suns relatively close together. If the map is produced to scale, those two dots can be used as a measurement yardstick. We can calculate this distance by observations from Earth and from that, work out the distances of the planet dots from the main star or sun (Perseus A) as in appendix 1.

And why are there two large dots among the row of planets? Obviously these must be interpreted as signifying the planets involved in the launching of the probe. In other words, the worlds of the Perseans.

If the Perseus A sun were the same size as our own sun, the first planet dot would be too far away to sustain life (nearly twice the distance from our sun to Earth). However, Perseus A was bigger and brighter than our own sun, and its radiation and warmth would have been quite sufficient to cover the extra distance and still provide the planet with the correct Earthlike temperature. Lawton has calculated that Perseus A—before it became a dying giant—would have been quite able to have planets suitable for living organisms. And its normal life span would be four thousand to five thousand million years—just long enough to create a highly intelligent species. He also estimates that the planet Perseus 1 moved around its sun in a 950-day year (more than two and a half Earth years).

The third of the five planets, Perseus 2 (again see Figure 7) is much farther away from the parent sun and would therefore be much colder, with a carbon dioxide atmosphere—like Mars. This planet's year would be 4,043 days, or 11.8 Earth years. (Details of these calculations are given in Appendix 1.) However, this second planet, Perseus 2, has a vital significance in the theme of this book. For although it is obviously colder and more hostile, the inhabitants of Perseus 1 would know that when their dying sun was incinerating their own planet, they could still move out of its deadly range by emigrating to Perseus 2, as a temporary escape before completely leaving their threatened solar system. How they would first make Perseus 2 habitable is explained in Chapter 9.

Let's now come down to Earth again for a moment. If there is an alien probe circling around us, and if we *are* able to let it know we have worked out the correct location of the intelligence that launched it, what would happen next?

We might suddenly get another sequence of quite different signals—this time just a series of regular dots (echoes), all with the same time interval. A mathematician, doodling in his notebook, might quickly recognize them as forming a binary number. If, for example, it was binary 7,850 and we had been transmitting on 31.4 meters—by dividing 31.4 meters by 7,850, we get 0.4 centimeters. And the probe could be telling us that it wanted to transmit its full information on a wavelength of 0.4 centimeters. At this wavelength it could even transmit television signals without difficulty.

We would then reply by transmitting back the binary number on the 0.4 centimeter wavelength—slightly varying it so that the probe would know just how much radio-band width it could use in its next—and most important—transmissions . . . television pictures, or digital pictures, as described in the previous chapter.

By this stage, what would now be a fully organized team of scientists on Earth would have erected not only a dish (antenna) receiver capable of working at 0.4 centimeters, but also video-tape recorders and television sets equipped with sophisticated decoding gear to produce a line and frame system as used in a normal TV receiver.

The first pictures we got might only be a series of all-black and all-white sequences—or possibly the Perseus solar system. This would be the equivalent of a TV test-card signal. To tell the probe we had received and understood a particular picture, we would simply transmit it back, together with a request for more information if required. The system, in computer parlance, is referred to as *addressing* and *handshaking*. It is a way of saying "Hello, I want to talk to you, and this is what I have got to say."

EIGHT

COULD THEY BE FLYING SAUCERS?

Could alien satellite probes account for some of the many flying-saucer reports over recent years? Could they be maneuvering out of their survey orbit to get a closer look at us—to make more detailed analyses of bustling Earth?

It is most unlikely. From the varied sightings reported from all over the world, few fit the logical, scientific conception of an unmanned satellite construction. Glowing saucers, rapidly moving lights, and cigar-shaped monstrosities are not the likely form a space probe would take. Its long-term surveillance job would require strict economy of power for only the most essential maneuvers. It certainly wouldn't be burning up its precious fuel bobbing to and from Earth from an orbit as far away as the moon.

So, if unidentified flying objects are not alien satellites, what are they? Do they, in fact, exist at all?

You have only to gaze out of the window of a railway carriage on a dark night and you'll see any number of glowing flying saucer and cigar shapes flittering past every minute—reflections from street lamps, neon signs, and other distorted stray lights from the other side of the track. Desperate travelers have witnessed nonexistent cases in the heat-haze of deserts throughout history . . . a phenomenon caused by the distortion of the sun's rays heating the desert air, which can make objects fifty or more miles away appear to be much closer.

Since a pilot named Kenneth Arnold claimed to have followed a geeselike formation of them in 1947, reports of flying saucers have poured in thick and fast all over the world. One, in 1966, was near a farm in Michigan. Frank Mannor, his son, and two neighbors found what they thought was a meteor. But as they got nearer they saw it was a flat dishlike object hovering eight feet from the ground. As they watched, they say, it began to glow and as they ran toward it, it vanished. They reported it to the police and later found that about fifty other people claimed to have seen it, including the deputy sheriff of Washtenaw County, who's reported as saying, "I saw it but I still don't believe it."

In one widely reported case at the Civil Aeronautics Authority traffic control center at Washington National Airport, the chief radar operator saw a number of strange objects recorded on the scanning screen. They were apparently doing the most incredible maneuvers —vanishing, reappearing, and varying their speed.

Airport controls around the area were asked to make a search and an operator at Andrews Air Force Base spotted a strange yellow light at one of the radar-defined spots. That same night pilots were asked to check the areas and two of them claim to have seen unusual objects.

Most observers claim UFOs are either silent in flight or give out bleeps, hums, or whirring sounds. They are usually disc-shaped, can hover or move instantaneously in any direction at speeds ranging from zero to that of our fastest rockets—with acceleration rates that would probably kill a human being instantly. Whenever a national paper records one, a spate of other reports inevitably follows.

In the last few years there have been various accounts of ground being scorched, crops incinerated, and odd indentations in the earth. It seems likely that most would have been caused by lightning, or simply by some local joker who could have set up the whole thing. In one incident in 1973, a farmer in Clarion, Ohio, found a forty-foot-wide area of his bean patch scorched, with holes about a foot across at each corner. A year before, a similar discovery was made by a farmer in Goldfield, fourteen miles away. UFO researchers claimed there had been many sightings in the area in 1972.

According to press reports in October 1972 at the village of Montauroux in the south of France, more than three hundred square yards of pine and white oaks were found to be flattened by some mysterious force. A drystone wall had exploded in all directions. A thick tree trunk had been unrooted and hurled several yards, and pine trees eighteen inches thick were said to have been twisted in different directions and curled up. Police and scientists were unable to explain any of it, but the villagers were convinced that only a flying saucer could have caused such havoc.

A professor of mineralogical research from Nice University who studied the soil and rocks was quoted: "Nothing in the arsenal of my knowledge enables me to explain this phenomenon. The cause was definitely not a meteorite, and a whirlwind always turns in the same direction. These trees were twisted in different directions." A biology student is reported as finding that his compass "went haywire" at the spot, and pointed due west instead of magnetic north.

In the autumn of 1973 a fresh outbreak of saucer mania swept some American states. Some of the sightings, from a flood of them received by authorities in Alabama and Georgia, were reported by police officers—though none of the "sightings" showed up on local radar networks.

Most were described as noiseless, rapidly-moving oval-shaped objects with colored lights. In fact, two military policemen claimed that a saucer-shaped object buzzed their patrol car at a hundred miles per hour and ran them off the road. One of the officers is reported as saying: "I could hardly see through the windshield because of the red and white flashes of the saucer's lights a few feet above us."

His colleague said that he was so terrified *he* crouched under the dashboard. "The object couldn't have been more than a couple of feet above us," he said, "and I reckon it was fifty to seventy-five feet across." After their car swerved onto a grass verge, the object was said to skim off into the distance.

There have been a number of claims by people who insist they have actually met aliens and even been taken aboard their spacecraft. The best-known account is that of a New Hampshire couple, Betty and Barney Hill, who told of their dramatic encounter in John G. Fuller's book *The Interrupted Journey*. They described how humanlike creatures with widely spaced oriental eyes and no bridge to their noses, interrogated them and even scraped some skin from Betty Hill's arm for tests. She says that there were instruments and solar maps in the spaceship.

In October 1973 the *New York Post* followed up a similar report from two Mississippi shipyard workers by quoting Professor Allen Hynek, chairman of Northwestern University's astronomy department, as saying: "They're not crackpots. There was definitely something here that was not terrestrial."

The Mississippi shipyard workers, Charles Hickson, forty-five, and Calvin Parker, nineteen, from Pascagoula, told how they were fishing on a river pier when a blue-colored craft appeared and three creatures floated away from it. They had wrinkled skin, sharp noses with holes beneath them, slitlike eyes, and pointed ears. Hickson and Parker said they were taken aboard the strange craft, examined, and released—just as the Hills had been in 1961. Three other people in the Pascagoula area reported seeing UFOs that night.

A few days later Dr. James Harder of the University of California Engineering College at Berkeley, and consultant to the Aerial Phenomenon Research Organization in Tucson, Arizona, examined both men under hypnosis, together with Professor Hynek. The *New York Post* quotes Harder: "It's not a hoax. It's an entirely real experience they had. There is no room for ridicule in this case. I was able to regress each of them into the experience. Their reaction of fear and terror was evidence to me, beyond reasonable doubt, that they were reliving an experience."

The younger man, said Harder, lost consciousness when he was taken aboard the craft and could not give a complete account, though "the older man retained consciousness, but he was so terrorized that I had to break off the hypnotic experience at a point where it became too painful to him."

Most serious students of these intriguing phenomena are quite convinced that in a great number of cases reported over many years (it is certainly not a controversy exclusive to the twentieth century) some people actually *have* seen flying saucers, cigar-shaped spacecraft, and glowing lights in the sky. I am equally convinced.

I am sure that those witnesses I have interviewed were quite sincere in the accounts of what they saw, or believed they saw. But then, after months of investigation into psychic phenomena, I am also convinced that people "see" ghosts. I have never seen one, nor have I ever seen a flying saucer, but the odds are that ten percent of the readers of this book will faithfully claim to have seen one or the other.

So, are earthly apparitions and flying saucers manifested in the same manner? And if they are, do they exist or don't they?

In October 1973 one of Britain's leading medical journals, *The Lancet*, published a revealing series of tests into the mental, psychological, and physiological problems and stresses of a group of men and women who took part in the 1972 transatlantic yacht race.

Thirty of a total of fifty-five, including five Americans, who endured the grueling three-thousand-mile single-handed crossing from Plymouth, England to Newport, Rhode Island, filled in daily progress cards accurately recording their physical and mental reactions during the voyage. They were also later interviewed by the man who organized the survey, Glin Bennet of the University of Bristol in England.

Some remarkable things happened to them. Apart from forgetfulness and navigational errors, they had vivid auditory and visual hallucinations. They saw and heard strange things that just did not exist.

Most were deprived of sleep during the race, which lasted from twenty to fifty-eight days, with some stragglers taking up to eighty-eight days. They were all basically clear-thinking, practical people of varied professions, including a bank manager, dentist, pharmacist, architect, and lawyer.

What happened to many of them would have under normal circumstances been clearly regarded as "evidence of severe mental disorder," writes Bennet. Yet, taking into account the punishing storms, fogs, icebergs, and the frustrating calms and long, lonely hours at helm, often cold, seasick, and hungry—what happened to them must represent normal reactions . . . things that would have happened to any of us. And some of the things that occurred were quite bizarre, including premonitions, wild dreams, and hallucinations.

One of the most startling was that experienced by a yachtsman after thirty-three days at sea. He spotted what he thought was a baby elephant just below the surface of the water. "A funny place to put a baby elephant," he mused. Then he thought it was a small family automobile. It actually turned out to be a whale.

After twenty-six days of sailing, another man recorded: "While at the helm last night I saw what looked like the reflection of a window moving about twenty feet below the surface. It passed me three or four times." A third lone navigator clearly saw his father-in-law at the top of the mast. Later that same evening he looked down into the cabin and saw his wife, then his mother, and then his daughter, lying on a bunk.

A number of them heard voices. One listened to high-pitched cries of "Bill, Bill," coming from the rigging and another "got spots before my eyes when looking at the sky" and made errors in navigation and sail handling. The difference between the states of sleeping and waking were often blurred and one man wrote: "My mind was completely separated from my body. I just used my body to get me around the boat and eventually there was no difference between sleeping and waking . . . almost like being drunk or high on pot."

Three people reported having strange premonitions either while awake or asleep and felt someone shaking them and calling to them to get up. Five days out, according to one of them, "I awoke from a dream with someone shaking my shoulder, telling me to get up and go on deck as there was shipping about, and not to forget to drop my wife off at Lugo [Spain]. I do not know who the figure represented, but I know it was a friend."

The calm periods caused great psychological strain on some. In one run of diary entries the word *becalmed* was written bigger and bigger on each succeeding page, until the word covered two full sheets and the pencil was driven right through the paper.

139

In all these situations, writes Bennet, there seems to be a progression up to what one would call a frank hallucination as the senses become more and more fatigued. The experiences were completely real to these people. A man who experienced someone else on-board certainly never questioned the reality at the time.

It is not uncommon for extreme and hazardous experiences such as these to bring on hallucinations. There must be many that would account for the strange and wonderful sea stories that are repeated at dockside taverns all over the world. From Bennet's survey, it is easy to understand how mermaids and sea monsters must have appeared so real to many a weary seafarer in the past . . . just as UFOs and other baffling phenomena must be so real to many people today.

It is easy to accept that some severe emotional crisis can unsettle even the most balanced mind into manifesting the subject of that crisis, such as a loved one who has died. And how many of those UFOs have been just the uncanny products of a tired businessman's mind, a frustrated housewife, a scorned lover, or a student up to his neck in advanced maths?

Stresses of this kind might even account for the most way-out reports—like one during the 1968 Buenos Aires epidemic of sightings of a saucerful of bald-headed dwarfs on a motorway. It led to traffic being held up for hours as police and drivers scurried around the area like distracted ants.

The many thousands of people who claim they see ghosts and UFOs (if these both belong in the same category) cannot all be cranks and weirdies. The vast majority of those I have met appeared sober, reputedly honest, down-to-earth individuals. Rarely did they seek publicity. They did not ask me to quote them and usually did not wish to be photographed. Only a handful had even the remotest knowledge of psychic matters.

So what they saw was either a mentally self-induced

confidence trick, a perfectly natural happening such as a mirage or the interplay of light and shade, or actual things that *did* exist in some form.

Can we seriously consider the last possibility? If things exist we can see and touch them. You can't put your hand right through a table or another person, as you're supposed to be able to do with a ghost. But what about a puff of cigar smoke? That exists and yet you can put your hand through it. Both the table and the puff of smoke are real enough. They are both composed of groups of atoms and molecules. They are both physical things.

All matter, including ourselves, is composed of countless numbers of atoms, and only a tiny fraction of an atom is solid matter—the proton and the electrons that spin around it. The rest of the atom, virtually the whole of it, is space or confined energy.

So, if most objects, including ourselves, are composed mainly of space, it is not too inconceivable that if, for example, some magnetic force could change the energy pattern of different masses of atoms, those masses might interlace so that one mass would pass right through the other. Or to bring it down to common objects—that your hand would pass right through a tabletop.

Many psychic students believe that something of this kind does occur; that a certain force generated from a human mind can cause changes in the energy patterns of objects and physically affect them in some way.

Some researchers claim this kind of mental force can even move solid objects. The remarkable case of a young Israeli, Uri Geller, who is reported to bend metal objects without touching them in any way, is discussed in Chapter 11.

One theory is that UFOs and Earthbound psychic phenomena are in existence around us at all times. The fact that most of us cannot see them, researchers argue, is no proof that they are not there.

Consider electromagnetic waves. They are continually present in our everyday lives. But we can't see them and we can't hear them—*until we switch on our television or radio sets*. We then know they exist, because our receivers have been able to tune in to the corect wavelength frequency to manifest them into real pictures and real sound. If our own brain—the most sensitive receiver of the lot—could be attuned to the correct frequency, might there not be all manner of sights and sounds around us?

"I'll believe it when I see it," is the common response of the cynic. But just how much can we see? Light, like sound, is composed of wavelengths which each register as a different color of a broad spectrum. As with sound waves, a receiver tuned to the appropriate frequencies makes those colors, or rays, visible. Our eyes are such receivers. But their normal range of frequencies is very limited. They just cannot register the further ends of the spectrum of light—where it is composed of such forms as infrared (heat), ultraviolet, gamma rays, and X rays—any more than our ears can register extremes of sound, such as ultrasonic, which are well beyond our natural frequency range.

So, if we are enveloped in energies that our usual senses limit us from experiencing, might flying saucers and ghosts—if either exist—be somehow mainly confined to some section of those extreme frequencies of light and sound so that in our normal state, and with our minds normally attuned, these objects would be silent and invisible?

Can the human mind occasionally cross over those limits? Or, alternatively, do those sights and sounds of another frequency or dimension cross over into our own? Perhaps some extraterrestrial intelligences have acquired the art of switching over from one dimension to another—a maneuver that might explain how UFOs are so often claimed to appear and vanish almost instantaneously. And maybe there *are* some human minds that can occasionally, accidentally or subconsciously, tune in to some of these normally out-of-bounds wavelengths.

Could the mysterious sightings be from a dimension entirely different from our own? Author Kenneth Gatland, in his book *The Inhabited Universe*, describes some thought-provoking effects of hypothetical encounters between intelligences of different dimensions. Imagine, he says, stepping into a looking-glass world of only two dimensions, which he calls Flatland. The inhabitants would be as shadows, having only length and breadth. Despite their high intelligence, these creatures would possess absolutely no knowledge of any other dimension—no conception of depth or height, of rising or falling. Their world would be like a vast, flat sheet of paper.

"Consider what would happen," he says, "if a sphere (representing our three-dimensional world) were to descend upon the plane of Flatland and pass through it. Lacking any conception of three-dimensional space (like ours), the inhabitants of Flatland would not see the approaching sphere, nor could they have any idea of its solidity. They would be aware only of the impression of a circle, which grows from a point as the sphere cuts the plane of Flatland, driving them out from its circumference. The circle would continue to expand until half the sphere had passed through the plane of Flatland, when the circle would begin to contract, diminishing again to a point and vanishing as the sphere departed.

"How would the Flatlanders regard this phenomenon? No doubt many would regard it as a kind of miracle. The Einsteins of Flatland would have a number of ingenious theories, though none of them would have any chance of comprehending the truth. They would be able to measure the rate at which the circle expanded and contracted and would mistakenly attribute to *growth in time* what the more privileged observer in three dimensions ascribes to *solidity and motion*."

How then can man possibly comprehend a four-dimension world where the past and the future both exist together and would be perfectly observable to an intelligence that was part of that world? Don't we get very near to a situation such as this in our dreams? Perhaps, continues Gatland, all dimensions are dream worlds. Might our world that seems so solid and tangible to us, be—like space and time—pure manifestations in the limited consciousness?

And might not universes of four, five, and more dimensions all coexist? Each would be distinguishable only by its own particular wavelength, so that only the correct type of consciousness, or receiver, could attune itself to become aware of, and comprehend, that world.

Author Maxwell Cade has made references to remarkable examples of astrological influences on humans, such as reports of a significant relationship between magnetic disturbances of the sun and the number of psychiatric patients admitted to hospitals. In his discussions with many doctors, he found further evidence of this phenomenon.

In 1964, Dr. Marcel Poumailloux, secretary of the World Medical Association, told a meeting of the British Medical Association that he had found a remarkable corelationship between sunspot activity and heart attacks, and one of his suggestions was that cosmic particles could in some way be causing blood clots. The nearest supernova explosions in the galaxy also increase the intensity of cosmic rays reaching Earth and are immediately preceded by a stage when they radiate a vast amount of X rays and neutrinos, which are also thought to effect humans and animals. Cade noted that supernova explosions in 1572 and 1604 were both immediately preceded by large increases in the death rate, attributed at those times to various forms of plague.

In 1972 the giant Palomar telescope began a deep supernova-search program. The results, published late in 1973 by the Astronomical Society of the Pacific, showed thirteen of these spectacular explosions in various galaxies. Another twenty-four were spotted after scrutiny of photographic plates from a previous survey.

Many books have been crammed with reported sightings of UFOs and with various forms of supernatural experiences. A fraction of the more unusual ones still gets space in the press. Most of those that get as far as the news editor are rapidly impaled on the throw-out spike. So I will simply deal with a few examples of various claims and viewpoints I have personally encountered over the last few years as a newspaper journalist. From the many flying-saucer sightings I shall merely record one that is typical of so many reported year after year.

At five minutes to midnight on October 9, 1972, police security officer John Byrne, aged forty-four, was making his check-up round of a large electronic engineering depot in Lancashire, England. It was a clear, still, and starlit night. Then, he told me, the following occurred: "As I walked back to the factory I was suddenly aware of a low, humming noise, like a generator. I looked around. I knew there was no machinery working at the factory, which was empty.

"I then looked to the sky and saw this object. Believe me, it really was massive. It terrified me and I never want to see anything like it again. It wasn't moving. It was just hovering at, I would guess, around 250 to 300 feet and it appeared to be about 100 feet in diameter. From beneath, the object just looked like a very large disc with what appeared to be a window at the front. This had a bluey-white fluorescent light.

"After hovering there for about five minutes, it quite suddenly turned on its edge and I then saw that it was dome-shaped on the other side—like an elongated bell or helmet. It seemed to have a bluey metallic tint and I got the impression of bars of some kind across the dome section, which itself gave off a fluorescent light. It hovered there for a moment on its edge and then took off, straight up into the sky, at an incredible speed. Within seconds it had vanished.

"I reported it to police headquarters and also to the radio telescope center at Jodrell Bank, which asked for drawings and specifications. An architect did these for me."

There was another witness of the saucer that night, from a fourteen-year-old schoolboy. His story was basically the same as John Byrne's, whose report he claimed to have been unaware of.

John Byrne appeared to me to be a perfectly level-headed police officer. He had never reported an experience of this kind before, nor, to my knowledge, has he done since. He does not drink and he does not believe in the supernatural. I believe he saw what he says he did. But was it pure imagination; was it some manifestation of energy or was it, in fact, really something solid?

Now take a comparative situation, but this time we substitute the flying saucer with two little old ladies. One young couple of newlyweds from the same town as John Byrne saw—or thought they saw—just that. And their type of experience is typical of many thousands reported in America and other parts of the world.

When in 1972 a local estate agent offered Brian and Bernadette Dunleavy the key to a small, terraced house, they jumped at the offer. Homes were in desperately short supply and nothing, declared pretty nurse Bernadette, would have induced them to leave it.

But something did. Soon after they moved in, they told me, noises of crashing crockery, stamping, and crunching sounds began to wake them at night. Lights switched themselves on and off. And finally they rushed from the house in terror when, they claimed, the forms of two grinning old women suddenly appeared on the settee. Badly though they had needed the house, they have not returned since that day.

I have investigated many cases similar to the Dunleavys' and, of course, could get no closer to any kind of logical explanation for them. But I do not believe they were deliberately lying to me. They were, I'm convinced, faithfully recording what they saw, or what they thought they saw, just as the majority of sincere UFO witnesses have done.

One theory of psychical researchers—perhaps not so far removed from the accepted Einstein laws of relativity—is that everything and every event in the universe exists permanently in its own dimension of time and space. These events, they suggest, might have been recorded on some kind of psychic film or tape which plays itself back from time to time.

Whatever these various phenomena are, an incredible amount of serious scientific study is continually going on throughout the world. Some groups of researchers are now using the latest electronic equipment in their dedicated pursuit of some tangible proof one way or the other.

Armed with tape recorders, electronic thermographs to register temperature changes, intricate vibration detectors, infrared photographic gear, and highly sensitive equipment for decibel readings, they are ready to spend months at a time studying a single report. They examine the psychological makeup of the people involved. They eliminate any obscure natural cause, such as loose floorboards and land subsidence, which have been known to cause light switches to operate. They look deeply into the history and geology of an area from references in local libraries and universities. And eventually they build up a complete dossier of the situation. Most have a scientific explanation—like the strange case of *the dagger on the wall*. . . .

A young couple reported that the perfect image of a dagger appeared on a wall of their home whenever they switched on an electric light in an adjoining room. It appeared to be reflected from an old wall mirror.

147

Police, spiritualists, priests, university students, and newspapermen came to see it; none could find anything odd about the mirror. The priest duly sprinkled holy water on it, which made no difference.

A research unit investigated. They took the mirror from the wall and pointed it to the ceiling. Instead of the dagger shape the reflection produced two concentric circles. As they turned the mirror from the flat plane of the ceiling back to the vertical plane of the wall, the circles became elongated and began to cross each other until eventually they again formed the precise shape of a dagger. The reason? Within the thickness of the mirror itself were hairline cracks which could not be seen. A Newton's rings* effect was being produced.

Similarly, examples of exhaustive detective work are carried out when particularly strong evidence of UFOs is reported. One such sighting was actually photographed by a woman with a motion-picture camera onboard a plane taking off from England. When she projected her developed film, the family gathering was staggered to see a strange object suddenly appear on the screen, hover for a few seconds and then vanish. It was sausage-shaped and moved at such a rate that experts said it would have required phenomenal acceleration to perform such a maneuver. Immediately the press ran headlines of flying saucers.

Investigators then asked the woman passenger if she had panned, or swept, her camera across the aircraft window. She had, and this gave them the explanation of the UFO. From the angle at which she had been sitting in the plane, the balance weight on the end of the aircraft elevator was just visible near the edge of the window. When the camera was panned through this angle, the balance weight took on a distorted shape—

*Newton's rings are colored rings due to light interferences that are seen about the contact of a convex lens with a plane surface or of two lenses differing in curvature.

the sausage shape shown on the home movie. Since the illusion was only visible over a small angle, the object seemed to move very fast indeed.

The theory was proved later by mounting another motion-picture camera in the appropriate aircraft seat and swinging through the same angles as the woman had done. Sure enough, when the film was projected, there was the same shape moving in precisely the way it had on the home movie. To complete the test, another shot taken with the camera held firmly at the same angle "froze" the shape, and it showed up quite clearly as the balance weight.

Many flying saucer sightings over the last ten years have resulted from high-powered xenon arc lamps now carried by modern aircraft. These produce a brilliant blue-white light visible over forty miles. They can look exactly like a bright star traveling very slowly, and, due to deceptive perspective, can appear to be at a low altitude. In addition, these lights can be pulsed, or coded, to flash on and off very rapidly, like an airborne lighthouse.

Back in 1953 Anthony Lawton was with a research team which, led by the eminent Sir Barnes Wallis, was developing the world's first swing-wing aircraft (work that eventually led to the present F-111). They were using an isolated ex-Royal Air Force base in Cornwall, England. When test flights began, the strange and unorthodox shapes of those pilotless, radio-controlled craft sweeping across the Cornish countryside led to a flood of flying saucer reports.

They were propelled by liquid-fuel rocket motors that could be switched on and off in flight. When off, the aircraft glided with an eerie moaning sound as the air passed over the unusual body shape. When the rocket motors were switched on, the craft would leap forward with a screeching roar, terrifying people who had no idea what they were. Flying saucers seemed, to them, the obvious answer—and it made a useful security cover for the real top-secret work Lawton and his colleagues were doing. In fact, a popular science-fiction novel—later made into a film—emerged from the whole bizarre situation.

"But," says Lawton, "there was still one report out of the many that poured in during that time, that neither I, nor anyone else, has ever been able to explain. One day radio operators from a nearby Royal Navy station rang to ask if we were conducting trials. They had radar-tracked an object flying at fifteen hundred miles per hour which was on a steady course that took it straight up the English Channel. It had been under radar observation for several minutes.

"Trials were *not* being carried out that day and our aircraft were certainly not capable of such speeds or altitude and range. And yet something *had* been seen—by qualified radio operators using professional equipment—which could not be accounted for. It was not a swing-wing aircraft, it was not a radar fault—it was a true UFO."

According to the U.S. Air Force UFO investigation team, out of a thousand sightings that were checked each year about 2.5 percent could not be explained away as natural phenomena. The rest were usually such things as the moon or stars seen through cloud or haze, Earth-launched satellites, weather balloons, ordinary aircraft shimmering in the sunshine or, most common of all, the planet Venus seen in daylight.

But there are even more subtle forms of visual deception. The eye does not see like an ordinary camera. It operates like a television camera connected to a sophisticated computer. The computer (like the mind) is programmed to accept certain shapes, sizes, and forms. If the television camera saw an unusual, unprogrammed object, the computer would stretch its memory and come up with the nearest likely object within its experience. Almost certainly it would be wrong, and the identity it attached to the object might appear quite ridiculous.

In the same way, people observing what may be

perfectly natural—but absolutely unfamiliar—objects can only associate them with the nearest thing in their minds, which, with all the brainwashing press and television stories of UFOs, usually turn out to be "flying saucers."

The brain can actually be stimulated to see and hear things which definitely do not exist at the time. Often they are retained visions of some previous happening. It is not even necessary to have personally experienced that happening. A person could have been told about it or read about it—perhaps through a ghost story or, in the case of a child, a fairy tale. It is quite possible to immediately conjure up an imagined version of the event. However, as they would normally know, or have been told, it was only a story, they would not physically see it with their eyes. It would merely be a vision retained in the memory.

It has been shown, however, that if the appropriate part of the brain is stimulated by first exposing it and then touching it with a minute wire carrying a small electrical current, these images or visions can actually be seen as though they were really taking place. This method of artificial brain stimulation, pioneered several years ago, can affect a person's hearing and cause them to remember a piece of music or snatches of conversation, and is now a recognized technique for brain study and the treatment of amnesia, or loss of memory.

Research of this kind raises the possible theory that sights or sounds that do not exist—which might include UFOs and ghosts—can actually be created by an observer who may happen to be in an electrical or radio field of some sort. In fact, radio transmission may not necessarily have to be specifically directed at a subject to provide the required brain stimulation.

Natural radio fields can be generated by flashes of lightning. Overhead grid lines can also produce radio fields in wet or foggy weather, and people who live near high voltage electric cables will confirm that in rainy weather they get very poor radio and television reception and can hear the sizzling of the insulators coming over their sets.

Many people report seeing flying saucers near overhead electric cables. They are being quite honest. But what they could be seeing are merely stimulated memory visions, brought about by the radio fields these cables are producing. And how many ghosts are seen during thunderstorms? All good ghoul stories take place on dark and stormy nights, and it may well be that at these times people with particularly sensitive reception have had their brains stimulated by the radio fields from lightning flashes. Their story catches on, and another local spook is born.

Doctors A. Frey, M. Messenger, and E. Eichert of Minnesota University have been able to prove that radio fields can stimulate the neurons of the brain without them first having to expose it by opening up the skull.

These scientists found that by directing shortwave radio-frequency energy at people, some of them could actually hear sounds—usually buzzing, clicking, or hissing, which seemed to originate from within, or just behind, their heads.

After further experiments the scientists were even able to create particular kinds of sounds in the heads of the subjects. By modulating the microwave source with pulse generators, they found they could produce such recognizable things as bongo drums, lawnmower engines, electric saws, knockings on doors, and the tapping of a pencil. They are now attempting to produce actual speech. But only a few people have been found to be suitable subjects for this type of experiment, which could explain why the average person does *not* experience psychical phenomena or flying saucers.

But what about so-called mass sightings of UFOs? The most likely explanations—apart from them being part of a clever hoax—is that one or two people in a large crowd will possess this radio frequency neural sensitivity, and *will* "see" or "hear" something. Autosuggestion and a deep desire not to be left out of things, will induce a few others to back up the sighting.

Magnetic and radio fields are also generated by sunspots, and reach a peak intensity on Earth in the well-known northern or southern lights—the polar auroras. Some people who live in areas where auroras are common can actually hear sounds at those times, but cannot define them. It is possible that they are being stimulated by radio-frequency fields.

Reluctant though many of us might be to abandon those schoolboy convictions of little green men from Mars, evidence against UFOs being *solid* objects *physically* buzzing around our housetops is now pretty overwhelming.

During the International Geophysical year, the heavens were scanned for months on end by thousands of observers with just about every type of astronomical instrument. Plenty of very interesting objects were found—but no flying saucers. And, if they are up there in such profusion, our vigilant astronauts should be spotting them by the score. But they're not.

These days space is being sifted with a toothcomb network of early-warning systems every moment of the day and night with highly sensitive detectors that can spot even the smallest of objects. One must, therefore, categorize any sincere UFO sightings as either hallucinatory, as some form of energy manifestation, or as objects that are not of our dimension and would therefore be real only to an intelligence that was part of that dimension—that is, attuned to it. One, I fear, has to rule them out as solid, honest-to-goodness spaceships.

Professor Allen Hynek, America's leading UFO authority, says: "All known items aside—what is a flying saucer? We don't know, and until we *do* know what they are, we cannot attribute them to the creations or visitations of alien intelligence." However, when recently asked if an alien probe orbiting Earth—such as the type suggested by Bracewell, Lawton, and

Duncan Lunan—could be accurately classified as a flying saucer, the professor replied: "It certainly could."

NINE

BUYING TIME

Having launched some five hundred probes deep into the galaxy, the Perseans would have known they must then wait possibly as long as a thousand years for the star-seeking results that could eventually be fed through their central computer complex.

But they would also have realized that their beloved planet could not possibly survive that long. The ruthless inevitability of destruction by the very star that had given them life, must, they would have known, occur within the next two hundred years. And though they would have developed interplanetary vehicles of a limited type, they would only be at the early stages of producing spaceships capable of those gigantic velocities—near the speed of light—that could whisk them off and away to new and distant star systems.

Somehow, therefore, they would have had to find a way to buy time. The obvious answer would have been to organize a shuttle service for their inhabitants—

in spacecraft powered by more conventional rocket engines—to set up short-term tenancy on another planet within their own solar system, yet remote enough from the sun to escape its white-hot kiss of death for a few centuries longer. An overspill world that could feed and shelter their chosen colonists until the prying fleet of wandering satellites found permanent worlds for them outside their own system, and until they had finally developed techniques for interstellar travel.

Their target would have been the sister planet we shall term Perseus 2—more than three times the distance from the threatening heat of their swelling sun than Perseus 1. There, life could have existed for some centuries after the incineration of Perseus 1 had taken place. But, to enable their race to survive on this dead and desolate world might have meant drastic reshaping of its environment.

Many other worlds in our galaxy must have already moved on in this way. There seems no doubt that throughout the bustling universe advanced societies are, at this moment, actively engaged in colonizing other planets within their systems, just as our own bulging cities on Earth are spreading their industrial and residential overspill farther and farther into the rural countryside.

In some instances these "takeover" planets will have been completely reformed in advance of their new residents. Atmospheres will have been reconstructed to produce an environment in which they can live and produce their own kind of food, energy, and other resources. In some cases, where nearby planets are unsuitable or too costly to reform, artificial dome-type settlements with efficiently controlled environments will probably have been established.

In the case of a civilization which, like the Perseans', was escaping from solar destruction, one of these domes would be installed on their home planet, before they left it, as a research center. Heavily armored against growing radiation, its purpose would be to record the awesome bulge of their dying sun, until the moment came when even the massive protection measures could no longer ward off the intense energy.

One day man himself may be forced into a desperate escape-or-perish scheme such as this. Not because of extinction by the sun, for this is unlikely to come about for some thousands of millions of years, but by the progressive elbowing of overpopulation and shrinking resources on Earth.

What, therefore, would be man's galactic-overspill plans? Where would he choose to go, assuming it had to be within his own solar system?

The farseeing mind of Professor Carl Sagan, America's Cornell University, puts forward a remarkable scheme for colonizing Venus. But how, you may well ask, could man exist for even a moment on a hellish planet whose red-hot surface would grill him like an overdone steak at temperatures little short of 1000° F.

In fact, how could any living thing—no matter how resilient—survive beneath that permanent blanket of dense cloud whose mass of carbon dioxide produces the deadly "greenhouse effect" that pressure-cooks its environment by holding captive the remorseless heat of the sun?

The solution could be to somehow break down the poisonous Venusian atmosphere and so release free oxygen. Rain must then be induced to cool the planet's angry surface so that plant life could form, which would in turn use the sun's energy to produce the kind of photosynthesis that procreated life on Earth.

This, then, is Sagan's intriguing plan. First, a particularly resilient strain of blue-green algae would be bred over a number of years in laboratory conditions similar to those of the Venusian atmosphere. These would be the same tough little organisms that biologists believe were mainly responsible for extracting the carbon dioxide from Earth's first primitive atmosphere (in which present-day man would immediately choke to death) and replacing it with free oxygen.

Masses of these prolific algae would then be packed into the nose cones of small rockets. The rockets would then be loaded into an armada of manned spaceships which would encircle Venus in a series of interweaving orbits, firing into the atmosphere their rocket-propelled "bombs"—agents of life instead of those of death, with which man is at present so preoccupied.

As the rockets penetrated the deep Venusian cloud layer the nose cones would explode, releasing the algae into the atmosphere. There they would exist, reproducing just as others like them had done millions of years ago on Earth, breaking down the carbon dioxide into oxygen and carbon.

But one ingredient of the vital chemical process in the evolution of plant life would still be necessary. Water. As Venus is now, rainfall is quite impossible; it could never reach the hot surface before evaporating back into the clouds. However, unmanned American and Russian satellite probes have discovered that a very small amount of water vapor or ice-crystals does exist in the upper atmosphere of the planet.

So now, as the algae get on with their tireless task of replacing carbon dioxide with oxygen—and so breaking up the greenhouse effect of the dense cloud —the atmosphere would start to cool, water would collect in the clouds, and torrential rain would teem down.

The first downpours would, of course, merely vaporize into steam long before they hit the surface. But gradually, with each new refreshing torrent, the ground temperature would grow a little cooler and the carbon dioxide overhead would be broken up more rapidly. Finally, when the surface became perhaps a couple of hundred degrees, the heavens would open wide and the rain would cascade in surging fury across the thirsty ground, saturating it sufficiently to nurture the plant life that would follow.

Says Sagan: "The heat-retaining clouds will partially clear away, leaving an oxygen-rich atmosphere and a temperature cool enough to sustain hardy plants and animals from Earth."

The solar world planners of the future might consider Mars, too, as a possible overspill site. Two photographs taken by *Mariner 9* in 1972 now show evidence that water has existed on the surface of this controversial planet. Could there yet be some form of life already installed there? The photographs, reported the journal *Nature* in July 1973, show definite evidence of alpine glacial erosion in the south polar region occurring at some time in the past. U-shaped valleys and other glacial evidence closely resemble the ice-free features of the Cascade mountains in the northwestern United States. These valleys are separated by sharp ridges and channels that can only have been formed by the action of water.

However, a considerable drawback in selecting Mars as a readaptable world for man is that its puny gravity of three times less than Earth's would make it extremely difficult for any atmosphere to retain the elements vital to produce the kind of air that humans could breathe. But, if man cannot adapt Mars to sustain life of its own, there seems no doubt that by the end of the century he will have set up a space center there.

Once on this lonely moonlike world, teams of astronauts would set up laboratories on the pock-marked surface. And they may have to spend many long, cold, and silent nights there before they return to Earth. More researchers would follow until an entirely self-supporting colony had been set up.

America may have women astronauts by the 1980s as part of their space-lab project. After twelve years of opposition to the idea, space-agency chiefs have ordered a study into the best way they can be employed. Looking well ahead to the time when men and women set up bases together on planets like Mars, noted astronomer Patrick Moore poses some intriguing questions. Suppose a human baby was born there—would it ever be able to adapt to conditions back on Earth? Or would it become the first member of the first Martian race—confined to the forbidding planet for its entire life?

In August 1973 the publication *Nature* carried an exciting letter from American researchers claiming that they had detected ice caps on Europa—one of Jupiter's satellites. Europa, four-fifths the diameter of our own barren moon (which is devoid of surface ice and atmosphere) is Jupiter's second largest satellite.

The ice caps are said to cover about seven-tenths of it. The rest—about half the size of the United States—is open land, possibly with water vapor.

Until more intimate details of Europa are available, we cannot tell if the little world has life. But where there's ice there could be water. And where there's water there may be an atmosphere with winds to transport the ice, in the form of snowflakes, across the land. This icy atmosphere would almost certainly have been formed from volcanoes belching forth water vapor, carbon dioxide, and other gases, as was our own.

Volcanoes are powered by radioactive materials forming furnaces hot enough to melt rocks and other substances. One of the most common radioactive materials is potassium, which, on decomposing, gives off the gas—argon—which is heavy enough to be retained by the gentle gravity pull of Europa (only half that of the moon and one-thirtieth of Earth).

Under these conditions the chances of life could be certainly as good as that on Mars. Other observers are therefore being urged to study Europa—this minicompanion of the mighty Jupiter, five times as far from the sun as ourselves, and where the average 150-pound man would weigh only 5 pounds.

Perhaps over the next decade lander probes like

Viking might be settling their spindly legs on Europa to look, sniff, and scoop for those elusive signs of life.

Before an advanced race could undertake large-scale emigration over interstellar distances, its biologists may be required to actually change the genetic structure of their species to adapt it to conditions on other worlds. This kind of mutation may have to drastically change an individual's size, weight, and respiratory and circulatory systems—to produce massive lung capacities and gaping nostrils to take in a thinner atmosphere—or stouter, stronger limbs for a world with more powerful gravity.

They would also doubtless be highly skilled in a field already being studied by some scientists on Earth —the psychological influences on fetuses, or unborn children. They would be quite efficient at prenatal brainwashing procedures, whereby certain selected infants would be groomed to psychological suitability for space travel before they had even arrived into their anxious world. On a planet such as Perseus, those not chosen to perpetuate the race elsewhere would not have been permitted birth, for control of the population would, more than ever before, have been a vital part of Operation Survival.

At a conference in Germany in 1973 scientists urged that the "wonderful world" of prenatal life be opened up, saying that there were great possibilities for psychoanalysis during pregnancy.

The Perseans would also have been able to induce, before birth, special physical mutations in their chosen space travelers. These would ensure that they developed into extremely light, finely boned specimens to reduce the obvious weight problems involved in interstellar journeys.

Even Earth scientists may one day have to transform our descendants into these genetically malformed interstellar Frankenstein's monsters if we are forced to move outside of our own solar system.

161

Many of the most advanced extraterrestrial societies may have already moved far out to the very extremes of their galaxies as each of their colonies produced new ones to send to further new worlds in space. Eventually one single species of intelligent life might dominate an entire galaxy. It has been estimated that even man—still on the fringes of space exploration—could one day spread his colonies from star to star until he reaches the outer depths of the Milky Way, eighty thousand light-years distant, always sending on ahead his intricately programmed space computers to look over each new territory before his biologically adapted colonists move in.

Assuming that by that time our advanced technology will also have provided us with far speedier communication techniques, well-organized control of its mushrooming empire in space could be rigidly maintained from base-control Earth.

Though, perhaps, as time goes on Earth will no longer remain the capital of man's galactic domain. Perhaps an extraterrestrial Shangri-la will be encountered by some space-faring Christopher Columbus, brimming with vast untapped resources that will become man's new headquarters, leaving a few of the more hardy species of animal and insect life to inherit Earth.

With any kind of galactic commonwealth, man's chances of survival would be greatly enhanced, in fact could be virtually eternal the deeper into space he fans out his prolific species. The end of our world would no longer mean the end of mankind. Humanity would be safely rehabilitated and its vital scientific and sociological assets wisely deposited in those intellectual safety-deposit boxes of the worlds outside.

It would, perhaps, be comforting to think that after man has eventually been forced to abandon this pretty little Earth he—or some mutated version of himself—might one day decide to come back and start up here again. By that time the natural resources we are all now rapidly draining away might have been replenished into a second Garden of Eden for the return of its prodigal sons.

Dr. Conley Powell of the University of Kentucky, discussing galactic colonization in his paper "Interstellar Flight and Intelligence in the Universe," says: "It will, in time, give us the opportunity to obtain detailed data on an enormous number of technological civilizations, existing under a wide range of conditions. Today we have no knowledge of any technological civilization other than our own. And ours is clearly in a very early stage of development. Given enough data, however, we may develop a mathematical theory of sociology, the immense value of which is obvious."

America's second Skylab mission in 1973 showed that there is no medical reason why man should not survive lengthy space flights. Previously there had been considerable concern that weightlessness would cause gradual physical deterioration. Astronauts Alan Bean, Owen Garriott, and Jack Lousma found that these effects are only temporary. At first all three, like the previous crew, steadily lost weight, lost minerals from their bones, and suffered from the gradual deterioration of their circulatory systems.

But halfway through their two-month flight, they appeared to adjust to their weightlessness. They actually gained a little weight and seemed to become fitter than their predecessors, who were in orbit only half as long. Despite motion sickness during the first week, the crew was able to do far more work than had been expected of them.

One obvious problem associated with long-distance space travel is the storage of huge quantities of the oxygen, food, and water that each passenger would require for journeys lasting many years. The Perseans would have experimented with complex systems of recycling all waste products back into palatable food, drinking water, and oxygen.

In 1973 Professor Josif Gitelzon and his team at the Russian Kirensky Institute of Physics completed a six-month experiment on close-cycle life-support systems for long-term astronaut flights, which relied primarily on biological processes.

Four men spent six months in a dummy spacecraft designed by a biologist. It was comprised of four sections—the crew lived in one, the rest were filled with plant life. Special rapidly developing varieties of vegetables, such as potatoes, onions, carrots, lettuce, and cucumbers, were grown in artificial soil. Xenon lamps provided artificial sunlight. Wheat was also cultivated.

In addition to the plants absorbing carbon dioxide and giving off oxygen for breathing, the crew was able to exist on a varied diet of fresh vegetables and home-made bread, as well as the normal dried food.

But, though this system would be useful for active members of a space vehicle's crew, to utilize it for an immense number of passengers, such as would have been involved in the mass emigration of the Perseans, would be far too unwieldly.

One solution might be to transform nonoperative passengers into some state of suspended animation for the voyage, possibly by deep-freezing them. Their body temperature would be reduced to below-zero temperatures, so holding back all physiological processes. They would then be safely rejuvenated back to normal by slowly thawing them out.

Other methods might be to artificially induce a state of hibernation or hypothermia. In hibernation, commonly practiced by a number of Earth creatures, the heart beats more slowly and reduces the flow of blood to the body tissues. These animals, however, have an in-built mechanism to bring on and control this state of hibernation. The Perseans would most likely have successfully evolved synthetic organs to achieve the same results in their astronauts.

As in hibernation, less nutrition and oxygen is required by a body in a state of hypothermia, which

164

reduces it to an abnormally low temperature. Earlier experiments, which may have been found to dangerously affect the functions of the heart, would have been overcome by artificial means.

For some years experiments to produce suspended animation have been taking place here on Earth. Rats are reported to have been cooled to a body temperature of $-1°$ C., remaining in a state of death for sixty to seventy minutes. They were completely revived after being warmed up again by microwave radiation. It was found that respiration stopped at about $15°$ C., and the heart at $8°$. Other animals were supercooled to $-7°$ C., and less, then were reanimated and recovered completely.

In fact, in the 1960s in America, human corpses were deep frozen immediately after death in the hope that when medical science was sufficiently advanced the bodies could be re-animated and cured of the disease that killed them.

At present, in Los Angeles and New Jersey, 14 bodies are stored in stainless steel cylinders at minus 320 degrees Fahrenheit. To cut the high cost of the process, experiments are being made with "communial" cylinders.

TEN

THE LIGHT BARRIER

For the last few generations on Perseus 1, a ruthless system of birth control and euthanasia might have been carried out as the dying sun grew to monstrous proportions century after century. Death from the increasing radiation from this glowing red ball of fire peering over their horizon would have reduced their numbers even more.

The genetically adapted elite of the race would have been moved to the safest, most temperate region of their planet to prepare for their comparatively short journey to Perseus 2. Perhaps from an original population of something double that of present-day mankind, some half a million would be chosen for the overspill scheme.

Massive spaceships would then have shuttled them across to their makeshift home, where they would have had more time to plan the permanent emigration of a future race of supernauts who would eventually move out to other star systems. Before that day came, more drastic pruning would be needed to reduce their numbers to, maybe, a manageable three hundred thousand, requiring an interstellar fleet of around 150 superspaceships.*

Moving to their sister planet would have presented no real problems to the advancing technological range of this dwindling society. Many times in the past their astronauts would have visited Perseus 2, together with other planets in their solar structure. From their grand tours of their system, there would have been little they did not already know about each of these lonely outposts.

Once they had settled on Perseus 2, the real challenge would have been to step up their interstellar space-flight research to enable their scientists to produce vehicles with velocities approaching that of the speed of light. They would know that only in this way could their inhabitants be physically transported hundreds of light-years to the planets where they must eventually resettle.

Ancient theories that colonies of their people could simply be packed like laboratory specimens into massive, conventionally powered spaceliners—moving majestically like some grotesque interstellar ark through the galaxy for thousands of years—would have long been abandoned. The appalling psychological effects on the individual members of these drifting masses of "humanity," sustaining a morbid life-and-death link through centuries of interbreeding, would have been only too evident from their first journeys to their companion star. The answer therefore had to be in designing and building faster and faster spaceships.

What would have been the problems facing those scientists and technicians in their urgent race to narrow the gap between them and the magic, all-embracing

*Further technical details of probes and interstellar fleets are given in appendix 5.

speed of light? What would be their chances of reaching this astronomical time barrier? Let us consider their predicament within the horizons of man's current reasoning.

In any theorizing on space travel approaching the speed of light, it is absolutely essential to first consider some of the basic aspects of the revolutionary logic contained in Albert Einstein's Special Theory of Relativity, which he unleashed on an incredulous world back in 1905.

His golden rule of time and space declares quite firmly that no material object moving through the known universe can ever travel at the speed of light because, as it approaches that speed, its length would shrink to zero and the energy needed to move it would rise toward infinity.

The obvious interpretation of this theory is that clearly no body—such as a spacecraft—can possibly be of zero length (that is no length at all), nor can it have an engine of infinite power. So, therefore, no material object can ever crash the light barrier by sheer brute force.

Today, however, some of the world's most eminent astrophysicists are beginning to doubt this hard-line interpretation of Einstein and are suggesting that faster-than-light travel might be attained *without violating* his theory of relativity.

So, let us consider what would happen if, by some technological wizardry as yet unattainable, man does harness sufficient energy to blast a spaceship near to that mysterious barrier.

Again, to consider the exciting possibility, we must go back again to Einstein's theory. His reasoning is not easy to grasp. Our minds are essentially limited to what we can see and experience, and Einstein's logic goes far beyond that. Nevertheless it is essential that one thinks for a while on the broad implication of his theory of relativity before further considering the question of interstellar spaceflight.

First—the speed of light is constant throughout the universe. It can never vary. And it remains at precisely this constant speed regardless of any movement of the source from which it, or those about it, originates. That means that if a beam of light is flashed from Earth, the additional speed at which Earth is moving is *not* added to light's basic, unchangeable speed. It still remains constant at 186,000 miles per second.

This is quite contrary to our normal understanding of movement. If, for instance, a bullet was fired from the front of a car traveling at sixty miles per hour, the total speed of the bullet would be the velocity at which it left the barrel of the gun *plus* the sixty miles per hour at which the car was traveling.

Secondly, mass and energy are interchangeable (this is dramatically illustrated by the atomic fission and fusion that produces bombs).

Thirdly, the mass of a body actually increases with its velocity. This may sound quite unrealistic, but it has been proved in laboratory tests by speeding up the particles of an atom to near the speed of light. Their size has been found to increase considerably. Therefore, according to Einstein, because a body increases in mass as it gets closer to the speed of light, it could never reach that speed limit because it would, by that stage, possess infinite mass and, even by harnessing the total energy of all matter in the universe, it would be impossible to accelerate it any further.

Now, another thing would happen. Not merely would an object's mass increase at speeds approaching that of light, but so would its state of time. The reason for this, says Einstein, is that because all bodies in space have their own particular motion, each must have its own particular time scale. These differences are not noticeable at velocities with which we are accustomed, but consider what would happen aboard a hypothetical spacecraft traveling at near the speed of light.

Let us imagine we could observe it from Earth. Some startling things would be happening to those onboard. The ticking of the clocks would have slowed down to almost zero. The weight of the spaceship would increase and its shape would become flattened or foreshortened, in the direction it was traveling, to a fraction of the length it should be. The same thing would be happening to the passengers. Their breathing and heartbeats would have slowed down too. But, for the passengers themselves, everything would be perfectly normal. The time, their shape, their weight—everything.

Now, the staggering result of this time difference would be that if the spacecraft left Earth in 1974 and went to the nearest star, returning in 1987 by Earth time, the passengers would be only one year older than they'd been when they'd started off, due to this remarkable relationship between time as a dimension and the speed of light.

Astrophysicist Sebastian von Hoerner takes this bizarre situation further. The longer a journey was, he points out, the more extreme the time-speed effect, until finally time on the spacecraft would virtually come to a halt. He has, therefore, calculated that in a twenty-year round trip onboard the ship, including delays needed to accelerate and decelerate, a space traveler would return to a world 270 years older than it was when he'd left it. And after a sixty-year journey the astronaut would find the world a staggering five million years older. And he would have traveled some two and a half million light-years!

We have scientific proof of this slowing down of time at these incredible speeds. Nuclear particles, known as *mu mesons* or *muons*, are continually falling onto the surface of Earth. These particles are produced when atoms are smashed by high-energy cosmic rays. They plunge into our atmosphere from space at near the speed of light.

Now, the lifetime of a laboratory-made muon is known to be only 2.2 millionths of a second, and so, since they are generated naturally only in our outer atmosphere—at about ten miles up—they should disintegrate after traveling no farther than about half a mile, despite their high speed. And yet they *do* survive to reach Earth, and one has been caught on films which reveal their telltale tracks.

It is precisely because of their speed—near to that of light—that their lifetimes are extended, just as Einstein predicted seventy years ago. And if this happens with a muon, there is no logical reason why it should not happen to anything else—including ourselves. There have been other experiments which support this theory, but the proof we have outlined is the simplest.

In fact, it has been calculated that when the *Apollo 9* astronauts landed after traveling around Earth for ten days at the comparatively slow speed of seventeen thousand miles per hour, they were 450 millionths of a second younger than they would have been if they'd never left Earth.

At the fantasy speeds approaching that of light, even the tiniest scraps of dust would batter a space ship with frightening force. A meteorite the size of a pea would literally explode it. For even such a tiny object as that would smash into the ship with an energy level of about a hundred thousand horsepower. And this is assuming that such a spaceship got off the ground in the first place. The blast-off from, for example, a rocket powered by gamma rays, would completely destroy any life in the vicinity. The gamma-ray beam from a starship, if launched from Earth orbit, would nearly cut the world in half!

A really novel idea for mass emigration was proposed in 1961 by scientist Darol Froman, who at that time was involved in work for the Atomic Energy Commission. Not to be taken too seriously, he suggested that we take Earth with us. In fact, transform it into one magnificent flying machine by propelling it into another solar system.

Fusion reaction, using seawater as fuel, might, he said, provide the massive energy for this remarkable undertaking. We would, he surmised, transform hydrogen nuclei—plentiful in our oceans—into helium (the kind of reaction that produces the sun's mighty energy). Twenty-five percent of it would blast us out of reach of the sun's gravity. A similar proportion would maneuver us into an alien solar system, and the rest could be kept in reserve for our heating en route as the scientists shuffled our global spacecraft around the galaxy—leaving us all to carry on our normal lives with all the comforts of home.

We could either hitch our wagon to a friendly star's orbit, or just keep moving—replenishing our oceans every now and then by gathering water from planets —or interstellar filling stations—on the way.

One form of interstellar propellant is actually available now. It is the ion rocket, and is already being test flown by America, Russia, and Britain, mainly for steering satellites. The rocket motor could be used for leisurely voyages to the nearest stars . . . taking two or three centuries.

The ion rocket works rather like a gigantic television cathode ray tube. In a TV set, small particles—electrons—are sprayed from a special "gun" onto a fluorescent powder on the inside of the screen. The powder lights up from the energy given off by the particles.

Now, if we floated a TV set into space with a hole cut in the screen, these particles would fly out and away from the set, and, theoretically, cause it to glide gently in the opposite direction. However, in practice, the force would be too small to be noticeable.

If we built a much bigger TV "gun" and, instead of electrons, fired ions—which are atomic nuclei in an electrically excited state—the contraption would most certainly appear to drift in the opposite direction.

Basically, an ion rocket shoots a steady stream of ions into space, producing a gentle but steady thrust

173

on the vehicle. The particles are usually of mercury, or perhaps, a rare gas called xenon. They are accelerated by voltage, not heat, as in an ordinary rocket, and so the main power form is electricity, usually produced by a nuclear generator.

The ion motor is therefore extremely efficient and generates a great deal of power from a small quantity of fuel. But it operates this power at very low thrust, measured in thousandths of a pound—not millions of tons. Theoretically, the ion motor could operate for long periods, for there is little to wear out. In practice, their present life span is limited by cathode poisoning and erosion, which stops the mercury filtering through into the "gun."

Ion rockets can produce speeds up to five percent of that of light, but must still be limited by the quantity of fuel they could carry. But though they would still take centuries for worthwhile interstellar voyages, ion engines *are* available now and could well be used to power automatic reconnaissance probes to alien planets.

Expeditions outside our own solar system might later be powered by nuclear pulse rockets. With this rather startling system, a series of low-yield nuclear bombs would be detonated at the rear of the spaceship —buffered by powerful shock absorbers. It has been estimated that a rocket of this type, with a payload of a thousand tons, could reach a star ten light-years away in sixty years. Its takeoff weight, however, would be ten million tons.

There are two major snags with the space vehicles mentioned so far. They are too slow for great interstellar voyages, and they have to carry their own fuel. One of our present-day *Saturn* rockets would take sixty thousand years to get an *Apollo* to the nearest star. *Pioneer 10*, which flew past Jupiter, will pass near Arcturus in two million years—and Arcturus is only thirty-four light-years away. And to be fairly confident of finding inhabited planets, we must need

174

to travel at least a hundred light-years—preferably up to three hundred.

So we want a vehicle that generates enormous power, moves at speeds close to that of light, and *doesn't* have to carry its own fuel.

Such a "magic" vehicle does exist . . . though only, as yet, on paper. But that paper is packed with hard facts and figures. It's not cereal-packet space fantasy. This incredible energy-gobbling monster is called a *ramjet* (see Figure 8). Its mighty motors would generate not thousands of horsepower, but several billion billion!

In fact, the total combined horsepower of all the steam engines, and all the diesel, rocket, and jet engines built from 1760 to 1974 would not come anywhere near the staggering power produced by the motor of *one* ramjet.

And yet it is quite feasible that within the next hundred years man will produce such a galactic brute. Crude little forms of it sent Nazi "doodle-bugs" or "buzz-bombs" scuttering over London in World War II. More sophisticated types drive *Bloodhound*, the British aircraft missile.

A ramjet has the remarkable ability to develop more power as it moves faster. Basically, if a simple funnel-shaped scoop is moved through air, the air is scooped in and compressed, or squashed tight. As a result of this it gets very hot. If petrol is squirted into this hot air it burns, and the funnel is "lit up." The hot, burning air tries to escape. It can't go forward—there is already more air crowding in on it. So it goes out through the back of the funnel. In doing so it pushes the funnel forward.

More air is scooped in; more petrol is pumped in, and more of the flaming-hot mixture is shot out at the rear as it develops even more power. This goes on unless either the fuel runs out or the motor melts and bursts.

That's all very well, you might say, but there's no

Figure 8

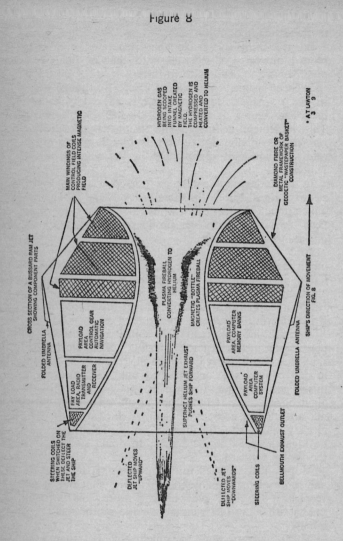

CROSS SECTION OF A BUSSARD RAM JET
SHOWING COMPONENT PARTS

MAIN WINDINGS OF
CONTROL FIELD COILS
PRODUCING INTENSE MAGNETIC
FIELD

HYDROGEN GAS
BEING SCOOPED
INTO INTAKE
FUNNEL CREATED
BY MAGNETIC
FIELD.
THE HYDROGEN IS
COMPRESSED AND
HEATED AND
CONVERTED TO HELIUM

FOLDED UMBRELLA
ANTENNA

PLASMA FIREBALL
CONVERTING HYDROGEN TO
HELIUM

DIAMOND FIBRE OR
METAL FRAMEWORK OF
GEODETIC "WASTEPAPER BASKET"
CONSTRUCTION

STEERING COILS
WHEN SWITCHED ON
THESE DEFLECT THE
JET AND STEER
THE SHIP

PAY LOAD
AREA, RADIO
TRANSMITTER
AND
RECEIVER

PAYLOAD
AREA
CONTROL GEAR
AUTOMATIC
NAVIGATION

MAGNETIC "BOTTLE"
CREATES PLASMA FIREBALL

PAYLOAD
AREA, COMPUTER
MEMORY BANKS

PAYLOAD
AREA
COMPUTER
SYSTEM

FOLDED UMBRELLA ANTENNA

SHIP'S DIRECTION OF MOVEMENT
FIG. 8

DEFLECTED
JET SHIP MOVES
"UPWARDS"

SUPERHOT HELIUM JET EXHAUST
PUSHES SHIP FORWARD

DEFLECTED JET
SHIP MOVES
"DOWNWARDS"

STEERING COILS

BELLMOUTH EXHAUST OUTLET

* AT LAWTON
3   9

fuel in space. Anyway, you've got to get the damn thing started. And won't it fizzle out, since there's no air in space either?

It's quite true there's no air in space, but there *is* fuel. At least there would be if you were traveling at high speed. In fact, there's plenty. It's hydrogen—the stuff of the stars, and the most common material in the universe.

It wouldn't be necessary to actually *burn* it, for if hydrogen is compressed enough it flares into helium. This is what the sun does. Or a hydrogen bomb. So, if an immense scoop was built and pushed through space, it would collect hydrogen. And if this were squashed hard enough it would produce helium and squirt the heated mixture out at the rear. The scoop would move forward and collect more hydrogen, which in turn would provide more helium to step up the speed.

This is virtually "riding the H-bomb." The practical difficulties are getting it started, making a big enough scoop, and stopping it from bursting once it *had* started. An additional headache is to "bottle" the hot hydrogen. Fortunately, a development in fusion reactors looks promising. A magnetic field could be made to bottle the hydrogen long enough for it to turn into helium and, if correctly devised, the field could also act as a scoop funnel. The man who first envisaged this idea was R.W. Bussard. Consequently, this type of space vehicle is often referred to as the Bussard ramjet.

Dr. Anthony Martin of City University in London is making a deep study of the problems of interstellar flight using Bussard ramjets. He has examined the stress limits on these spaceships built with materials available today. In a paper published in *Astronautica Acta* in 1973 he points out that a ramjet built of aluminum could withstand a journey of 12.6 light-years; in "onboard ship" time, 4.75 years. If the ship

177

were constructed of "patented steel (the strongest metal available) it could cover 120 light-years.

Now, if we were able to use diamonds to construct such a ship, we could travel an incredible thirty-five hundred light-years in an "onboard" time of 15.75 years. To man, at present, a diamond ship is, obviously, no more than a pipe dream. But real diamonds have been made in the laboratories of the giant General Electric and other corporations. One day our technology might actually spin diamond threads.

An advanced civilization like that of the Perseans would probably have been well ahead in this research, for they would be dealing with similar materials. The elements that we know of, and can now be manufactured on Earth, exist throughout the universe.

Carbon is a very common element—the essence of our life—and diamond is only a very special form of carbon. So, though a girl's best friend may be rare and expensive today, it will probably be easily manufactured fifty years from now. And, if it can be made as a thread, it can be woven to form a diamond-fiber composite. Bonded with a high-strength synthetic resin, a diamond fiber Bussard ramjet could travel those thirty-five hundred light-years in 15.75 years of "ship time" before its structure limited its acceleration.

Journey times of this magnitude could be made by using the normal thin spread of hydrogen between stars. If we consider operating near the hot stars or near nebulae which throw off masses of hydrogen, the ramjet would really begin to take full advantage of the effects of Time Dilation in Relativity, as outlined earlier in this chapter.

Dr. Martin also discusses these high hydrogen-dense regions. Here, because of Time Dilation effects, an aluminum ship would rapidly power-up and accelerate so fast that it would reach the center of the galaxy (Milky Way) in twenty ship years. A patented-steel vehicle would be able to streak right across it—

160,000 light-years—in twenty-five years and a diamond would flash over 3.8 million light-years in thirty ship years. This would easily take it to the next nearest galaxy (M31 in Andromeda), which is only half that distance.

The two dwarf stars that form part of Gamma Persei would provide ideal high-density areas for any Persean spaceships. They are close enough to each other to give not merely a hydrogen-rich atmosphere, but a supercharged bridge between them. However, a Bussard ramjet steered through this zone would need to be brought up to power gradually by slowly turning on the magnetic field. To switch on suddenly would burst the ship with the fury of an H-bomb.

How can man produce the intense magnetic fields needed to power ramjets? We already produce small ones by winding coils of insulated copper wire onto an iron core, similar to the choke or ballast used in a fluorescent lamp.

The magnetic fields we now produce are, of course, puny. But there is a class of materials (metals and alloys) known as *superconductors*. These have the remarkable property of possessing no electrical resistance at all, and an electric current set up in a coil of such material would last forever. Unfortunately these materials only have this property at very low temperatures (near absolute zero) and the best material must be cooled to $-250°$ C. before it superconducts.

Stanford University and several other research centers are investigating the possible manufacture of nonmetallic complexes that would be superconductors at more normal temperatures, but the work is only in its early stages.

Because superconductors have no resistance, colossal electric currents can be passed through them, resulting in intense magnetic fields without the need for those heavy iron cores. It is thought that one day these developments can lead to the large-scale confinement of hot hydrogen for fusion reactors to generate domestic power, gradually replacing the various types of fission reactors used at present.

Such a system could eventually lead to man designing the enormous magnets needed to sweep out the "crumbs" of hydrogen in free space and to channel them down the gaping throat of a ramjet, Dr. Martin estimates that for a reactor size of about ten feet, we may need an intake diameter, or magnetic-field sweep, as great as six million miles. However, for near stars—and certainly those in the Persean "bridge" zone—the required diameter would be far less and the input power to the magnetic field would be decreased.

The electrical power for this mammoth magnetic field would be drawn from the ramjet motor itself. Thus, a high level of motor power demands an intense field, which itself demands high power. The sensors and control equipment of such a system would have to deal rapidly with any variations in power output, for with such a basically unstable system, the motor could either burst or cut out. Again, the experience gained in power-station reactor development would be invaluable.

Finally, we would need to design a spaceship with the strongest possible structure for the minimum weight. The sturdiest shapes are circles or hoops and the interstellar ship of the future will likely be constructed like a gigantic wine glass bound together with a geodetic structure, making it appear rather like a wastepaper basket. The geodetic structure is the strongest linear construction for a given weight of material. It has been used by many designers of large domed complexes, such as sports' centers.

Contained in such geodetic structures, the starship of the twenty-first century would have coils of superconducting wire to generate the required magnetic field. It would also have cooling equipment to ensure that the wire *remains* superconducting throughout the journey.

The whole design—to include passenger and equipment areas—would be dominated by the monstrous circular intake, like a bell mouth. The exhaust system would be a slightly smaller bell shape. And both would have brilliantly polished surfaces to reflect heat from the main structure and back into the fusion inferno generated at the narrowest part of the bell "throat."

At the rear may be steering coils to produce small disturbing fields to offset the center of the fusion thrust and to swing the ship onto a desired course. The overall impression, therefore, of a great squat wastepaper basket will be far from the sleek, pointed starships of the schoolboy magazines.

Things like massive diamond starships are obviously far ahead of us. However, who knows, some technological whizz-kid may produce the "eureka" of the twenty-first century with an entirely new scientific law that will utterly demolish all our present theories of time, distance, gravity, and all the other apron strings that bind us to our maternal solar system.

But within our present techniques long-distance space travel must be strictly long term. And by astronomical reckoning, this could be in terms of centuries rather than years. Until someone shows us how to weave that interstellar "magic carpet" which must one day come about, our new breed of star-trekkers must develop a degree of patience as ample as space itself. The rest of society must be patient too, for it would be many, many years before their astronomical ambassadors returned to talk about their exploits.

Despite Einstein's law that it is impossible for any material body to even reach the speed of light, scientists are now considering a theory that subatomic particles, called *tachyons*, do in fact exceed this forbidden velocity. If man could achieve this also, would he then find himself in the timeless world of Wells, able to look back into the past?

Back in 1949 Dr. Kurt Gödel produced a fascinating paper claiming that it was theoretically possible

181

to travel into any region of time in the past or future, provided matter could be transformed into energy and a vehicle could be produced capable of 70.7 percent of the speed of light—or five hundred million miles per hour. His mathematical reasoning for this is far too complex to attempt to explain here. But its dramatic implications were discussed by D.F.A. Edwards in an article published in September 1970.

For instance, would the time traveler, or *chrononaut,* merely observe people and events in the past or future (including himself!) without them being aware of it? Or would the chrononaut actually be able to make his presence known, and even influence these events?

As mere observers of the future (and for all we know, writes Edwards, we may at present be under observation by posterity), we could take steps to prevent unpleasant happenings. And looking back into our own past would have great psychotherapeutic value "since we would observe unpleasant experiences that we have forgotten, but which still plague us from the depths of our unconscious minds. Psychoanalysis would then become extinct."

If, however, time travelers could actually be seen, would this explain the puzzle of the flying saucers as being visitors from time rather than space?

Edwards concludes: "While this article may at present seem farfetched, we should remember that as recently as 1956 the Astronomer Royal told the British press that space travel was 'utter bilge,' and in the 1930s one of the world's greatest nuclear physicists, Lord Rutherford, stated that man would never be able to make use of the power bound up in the atomic nucleus. If, then, Gödel's theory is correct and velocities approaching the speed of light become possible through advances in research and technology, then there is no reason why time travel should not become feasible."

Who, in fact, in age of such rapidly evolving technology, could now confidently proclaim *any* new idea to be impossible? How many traditionalists must have already bitten their tongues in the past after publicly announcing "It won't work!" Dr. L. D. Saegesser of the NASA Historical Office has collected some little "how-wrong-can-you-be" gems in what he calls his "Chronicle of Unhelpful Utterances." Here are some of them:

"The demonstration that no possible combination of known substances, known forms of machinery, and known forms of force, can be united in a practical machine by which man shall fly long distances through the air, seems, to the writer, as complete as it is possible for the demonstration of any physical fact to be." Simon Newcomb, *Sidelights of Astronomy* (New York, 1906).

"We follow with interest any work that is being done in other countries on jet propulsion, but scientific investigation into the possibilities has given no indication that this method can be a serious competitor to the airscrew-engine combination. We do not consider that we should be justified in spending any time or money on it ourselves." The British Under Secretary of State (in a communication, 1934).

". . . . A rocket capable of carrying a man to the moon and back would need to be of fantastic size and weight—so large, indeed, that the project could be classed as impossible. . . . The dream of human beings to fly to the stars must, as far as we can see, remain a dream." J. Himpan and R. Reichel, *American Journal of Physics,* 1949.

"Our candid opinion is that all talk of going to the moon, and all talk of signals from the moon, is sheer balderdash—in fact, just moonshine." Editorial answer to a reader's query in the *British Daily Mirror,* October 1948.

And finally—the summing up of Canadian astronomer Professor J. W. Campbell of the University of Alberta in an issue of *Philosophical Magazine* in 1941 was that it would require a *million tons* of takeoff weight to carry *one* pound of payload on a round trip to the moon.

What would an interstellar space flight be like for the passengers and crew of a starship capable of approaching the speed of light?

Unless the entire journey was computerized, navigation would be extremely difficult. Once out in space, beyond any atmospheric haze, the sky would be ablaze with stars. Even the dimmest would sparkle like diamonds. Against this dazzling array, star maps—those constellation patterns that would be the basis for interstellar navigation—would be almost impossible to identify. And as the ship accelerated and moved farther out of the solar system, the whole star scene would begin to change dramatically.

In a paper "Transtellar Navigation" James Strong, one of the chief engineers of Hawker Siddely Aircraft, speculates on what a journey might be like to the nearest star system, Centauri, in a super "Grand Prix" space vehicle of the future.

After traveling for about six weeks, the starship's velocity would be rapidly coming up to fifteen percent of the speed of light. This, he says, is what a passenger then starts to see:

The stars ahead would be brilliant but, looking back, all the yellow stars, including the sun, would have changed to orange. The red-dwarf stars would grow even duller until they were almost invisible. These color changes would be due to the Doppler Shift of starlight toward both ends of the spectrum as the ship speeds faster toward or away from each source of light.

"However," writes Strong, "by the time the speed has reached twenty-five to thirty percent of the speed of light (SOL), it will be clear that something else rather odd is happening to our universe. For instance, it will seem to the viewer as though the stars in front are steadily closing in, clustering in front as if to bar the way. The change is so stealthy as to be scarcely noticeable. Nevertheless, there are obviously more stars ahead than there were before. Meanwhile, star charts are rapidly becoming useless, as constellation after constellation is seemingly dragged forward, and distorted in the process.

"What goes on behind, as we look back, is equally disturbing. The stars are fewer in number, and those that remain—barely visible—are scattered and spread over a hemisphere that grows darker all the while. The sun has waned to an undistinguished, dull, red dot.

"The slow but steady and wholesale migration of the stars we are now witnessing is due to the aberration of light, a natural phenomenon that will become increasingly apparent as we approach relativistic speeds. In a way it is analogous to raindrops streaking the windows of a moving train. We know full well that the rain is falling vertically as we look out, yet the raindrops slant diagonally across the window, as if they originated from the top front corner. Similarly, the light from individual stars appears—when traveling relativistically—as though it is coming from some point ahead of where it really is.

"But there is worse to come. At thirty percent SOL, the light from the sun itself will have shifted so far into the infrared that it vanishes, to be replaced by a small, continuously expanding circle of darkness. At thirty-six percent SOL the light from Alpha Centauri likewise goes out. It too is replaced by a small, dark, and growing patch as Alpha Centauri's light is blue-shifted into the ultraviolet end of the spectrum, beyond the range of the naked eye.

"The vanishing of both sun and Alpha Centauri within a week of each other may well provoke misgivings among nonscientific passengers aboard. It could be allayed by showing them, via the medium of infrared and ultraviolet sensitive scanners, that both stars were still present and correct. The human eye, of course,

185

only responds to a narrow band of radiation in the electromagnetic spectrum."

The passengers would, of course, be witnessing an optical illusion on a grand scale, though it would look startlingly real.

Now, what happens as the ship moves even faster—to, say, half the speed of light? Human navigation would get more and more out of hand. The only visible stars would seem to be crammed together into a barrel-shaped arc around the ship. In this growing distortion it is doubtful if anything resembling a known constellation could be made out.

As the velocity increases even further, all the stars in the rear hemisphere would vanish. And finally, at ninety-nine percent SOL, the starlight ahead would form a complete, circular band of rainbow colors set in a background of total blackness. This effect is now referred to as a *starbow*.

The starbow is all a passenger would see until, as the spaceship approached its destination and began to slow down, all the stars would reappear and slip back into place. Once the speed fell below thirty-seven percent SOL, the target star would be dead ahead.

But, despite the obvious problems of navigating spaceships at these staggering speeds, there are systems already being used by man that could be adapted to cope with some of them. *Inertial navigation* is one. By this system—already used for missiles, nuclear submarines, and some military aircraft—a spaceship crew could determine their true speed and, theoretically, their location, by using a computer to compare the ship's accelerations with a suitable reference set at the start of the voyage.

Known spectral peculiarities of a reference star, such as the sun, could also help to maintain a navigational fix.

Included in a spaceship's navigation system would be a memory bank and a master clock. The memory bank would be the "ship's log." Initially, all the stars' coordinates and reference data would be fed into it, together with programming instructions for all system functions and voyage requirements.

Fixes would be checked daily, with monthly or even quarterly course corrections where necessary, and these too would be recorded and stored by the memory bank for further reference during the voyage.

The master clock would be vital, for upon its accuracy would depend the success of the voyage. It would read out "Earth time" and "ship time" (i.e. the crew's time), and would provide the information needed to determine speed and distances.

But possibly the most fearsome of hazards for interstellar travelers might be to encounter one of those dreaded black holes described in Chapter 2. These tiny, shrunken remnants of once-giant superstars are believed to have gravity fields powerful enough to destroy planets. Even a black hole with a nucleus the size of a grain of sand would have frightening destructive power.

In 1973 Doctors A. A. Jackson and Michael Ryan of the University of Texas at Austin suggested that a mystery meteorite which leveled hundreds of square kilometers of Siberian forestland in 1908 was, in fact, a black hole. Despite the havoc, no crater or remnants of a meteorite were ever found, even though the shock waves from the impact have been estimated at anything up to twenty megatons.

Jackson and Ryan speculated that a black hole landed in Siberia and drilled right through the earth, consuming a very small amount of rock in doing so, and emerging somewhere in the North Atlantic to continue its fearsome journey.

Had this black hole not passed right through us— had it stopped inside the earth—its phenomenal destructive power could have consumed us all. Scientists are now anxiously watching for evidence of any further visit from this tiny galactic vandal—possibly from dust encircling it or from the telltale bright blue jet that trails behind it. Let's all hope it gives us a wide berth. We might not be so lucky next time it calls.

ELEVEN

EXODUS TO THE UNKNOWN

For something like five hundred years—from perhaps our thirteenth to eighteenth centuries—the Perseans, now well-established on their new sister planet, would have been rapidly increasing their technology on a scale that might have placed them among the elite societies of our galaxy . . . even, maybe, in the *super-race* bracket.

During an era when Galileo was producing his first telescope and Isaac Newton confounding everyone with his astounding law of gravity, the Perseans might well have been harnessing godlike power from their sun—by this stage a gigantic, hungry monster that, even from their remote temporary world, was beginning to overwhelm them just as it had done on the now charred and lifeless remains of what had once been their home planet.

As our Western world was being enchanted by the leisurely genius of Shakespeare, Michelangelo, and

Johann Sebastian Bach, this eager restless civilization would have been urging on its most prolific scientific intellects in the frantic research so vital to the success of their emigration to the promised lands out among the twinkling jungle of the universe.

In fact, at just about the time the brave little *Mayflower* was leaving England for America with 102 intrepid pilgrims aboard, the travelers of a first interstellar Mayflower might well have been blasting off from a launching base on Perseus 2—prepared to face hazards and tribulations far vaster than those encountered by the New England settlers.

Their starship—possibly a ramjet—might have been streaking toward a pale pink band of light stretching between the two dwarf stars of Gamma Persei's minor component. For this would be their gateway to the universe . . . that power-packed hydrogen-rich zone that would give their ship the mighty spurt of energy to boost it on its long journey.

Perhaps that first party never even made the other side of that heavenly escape hatch. Perhaps they were spattered into space as their rocket motors burst into a catastrophic explosion, unable to take the sudden surge of power. Maybe they skirted too close to a star's inferno and were grilled out of existence.

But if these first emigrants perished even on their own solar doorstep, later ships would have gotten through. With precisely monitored maneuvers the computers would have guided them dead center past the two guardian stars.

There would have been many other hazards. Flares and solar storms would have caused dangerous "ebbs and flows" of hydrogen intensity as a ship passed through the "bridge"—like shooting some cosmic rapids. And sometimes two, or even more, journeys through it might have been necessary to acquire the needed departure speed of two to five percent SOL.

At this speed the motors would have developed about half of their full power, more than enough to ensure that the ship would reach the necessary speed in the lesser gas densities of outer space. A fearful moment of apprehension would have been felt as the computers onboard, being continuously fed with vital navigation data, finally nudged the ship into the correct path and switched on the magnetic fields to the required levels.

There would have been the ominous shudder as the fusion motors lit up and the ship gained speed, swinging back through the "bridge" and finally out into the void.

How many breathtaking plans, how many enchanting dreams went out with those Very Important Passengers as they watched the stars glow blue and bright ahead. What sophisticated schemes were filling their highly sensitive minds as their mother sun—the cause of it all—finally deserted them and faded from sight, lost in the fierce purple glow of the rocket exhaust.

And as they fled even faster they must have wondered what lay at the end of that magical rainbow effect that would have suddenly dominated the sky ahead as the computers, with their stern efficiency, flashed out the vital message "Starbow vertex angle cruise speed." From then on there would be no turning back.

Perhaps, like those other *Mayflower* travelers, they are destined to play just as significant a role in the future of some new, far-off world as was played by those dedicated pilgrim fathers in the life of American society three and a half centuries ago.

For contained in the computers and microfiles of their scientific baggage would have been the formulae and blueprints of unimaginable overspill schemes—including those to harness untold nourishment and power from the new stars to which their spaceship was heading. Schemes that would have enabled them to completely reconstruct the solar systems selected as future breeding grounds for their exalted race.

How could they have done this? How *could* a civilization capture and tame massive quantities of a sun's fervent radiation? Imagine what such an achievement would mean to mankind. . . .

Normally, a planet receives only a fraction of its sun's tremendous energy. Earth gets only a two-billionth of the sun's radiation. To meet its progressive needs, an advanced society might construct around a sun a gigantic sphere, with a radius of millions of miles, to collect and retain phenomenal supplies of heat and energy.

Implausible though such a colossal complex of astro-engineering might seem to us now, surely the building of the first spaceship to the moon would have seemed even more unthinkable to an ancient Briton, whose techniques were as far removed from ours today as ours are from a civilization such as that of the Perseans.

One distinguished scientist foresees this mammoth sun trap as mankind's eventual answer to our decreasing energy sources, and, in fact, goes even further with visions of entire galaxies "tamed" and tapped for their energy, matter, and living space.

He is Freeman J. Dyson, professor of physics at Priceton Institute for Advanced Study, a Fellow of the Royal Society and, among many other honors, has been voted the J. Robert Oppenheimer Memorial prize. A formidable intellect who predicts that interstellar voyages will begin from Earth two hundred years from now, the professor writes in one of his fascinating papers:

"It seems a reasonable expectation that population pressures will ultimately drive an intelligent species to adopt a more efficient exploitation of its available resources. One should expect that within a few thousand years of its entering the stage of industrial development, any intelligent species should be found occupying an artificial biosphere which completely surrounds its parent star. Indeed, if our own species continues to expand its population and its technology at an exponential rate, there may come a time when engineering on an astronomical scale will be both feasible and necessary."

Our sun, which is expected to stay as it is for the next five thousand million years, converts hydrogen into helium at a rate of something like four million tons per second to produce the overpowering energy that bathes its solar system. During the course of many centuries, Professor Dyson visualizes man constructing around the sun a partial sphere which would collect its vast energies in the form of radiation now going to waste in space.

But how can one even begin to contemplate such a project? Professor Dyson says we shall first commandeer the belt of asteroids—perhaps a hundred thousand of those tiny planets, or dwarf worlds—that are orbiting between Mars and Jupiter. Together, these chunks of rock would give our space contractors plenty of material to start with.

From this basic supply of orbiting building masonry would be developed an "open society" of space communities continually growing in number as do the suburbs of a large city—all orbiting in a sphere ninety-three million miles from the sun, just like Earth. Rocket engines would be used to shift the smaller asteroids into their correct places in the sphere. The larger ones (some are known to be more than four hundred miles in diameter) would be broken down with explosives before being nudged into place.

When the supply of asteroids runs out, there would be plenty of other available material in the planetoids and moons throughout our solar system. Special "factory" asteroids, designed to store heat, would be constructed in such a way as to restrain their normal rotation so that one side of them would always face the sun. In this way their temperatures would soar to thousands of degrees, so producing cheap, powerful energy that could be retained by the orbiting power stations. Century after century the sphere would continue to grow.

Now comes an even more staggering development in the Dyson plan as the search goes on for new material . . . the dismantling of one of the giant planets in the solar system. Breaking it up to form new space cities and miniplanets for the total population of human beings, which may, by then, be many thousands of times greater than at present. Dyson has published a fascinating paper, with detailed equations, on how this mammoth task could be performed over a period of forty thousand years.

The giant planet, he says, would be girded with metal grids at certain latitudes, like the armature of an electric motor. Concentrated solar energy from gigantic reflecting satellites would produce enough electrical stresses through these grids to accelerate the planet's rotation speed until it begins to tear itself apart by the centrifugal forces.

As the rotation increases, more sections would rip free into space until the once-proud and mighty planet would be just a gross collection of loose debri spinning around a tiny fraction of the original body.

A complete sphere would eventually be made up of millions of celestial objects, like a much thicker version of the ice crystals that make up the fascinating rings of Saturn. In fact, tiny, self-supporting worlds governed by the parent planet, Earth.

Dyson also believes that a densely packed orbiting sphere of this magnitude would be clearly detectable from civilizations in other parts of the galaxy, and that Earth astronomers should now be seeking evidence of these in addition to attempting to locate radio messages from extraterrestrial intelligences.

The eminent Russian scientist Kardashev has categorized civilizations according to the level of their technology. Earth, he says, is almost a phase I civilization, merely advanced sufficiently to utilize the energy resources of a single planet. A phase II society, like the

Perseans', would be able to draw on the entire energy of a star. Finally, at phase III, would be a race that would command the power resources of an entire galaxy. Obviously no civilization exists in our own galaxy that can have achieved this superpower, otherwise we would surely have detected it. But this does not rule out those thousands of millions of alien galaxies out there.

To achieve this final pinnacle of astroengineering, spheres would first be set up around neighboring stars, drawing material by systematically dismantling planets, until eventually the entire galaxy would be tamed to surrender its untold energy. Dyson foresees this super technology "moving from star to star in times, at most, of the order of a thousand years. It would spread from one end of the galaxy to another in ten million years—which is still a short time by astronomical standards."

Other reputable scientists are now openly contributing their own ideas to Dyson's wondrous vision of worlds without end. One suggestion, though not acceptable to Dyson, is that a powerful laser beam, fired at a star, could spark off a supernova explosion, expanding in a few days the star's total energy output, which would normally be spread over millions of years. The beam, working at gamma-ray frequencies, would deploy a million kilowatts (about a thousand times more than man's total power consumption), which would generate incredible energy as it struck the surface of the star. A nuclear chain reaction would then set up an almighty explosion.

Many astronomers who firmly regard these startling ideas as entirely feasible are today searching the heavens for any possible signs of a sphere such as Dyson portends.

However, rather than trigger a star into a supernova, Anthony Lawton suggests it might be possible to use less-powerful lasers to cause a particular spectral change, or signature, that would give a signal which other civilizations would immediately detect as a stellar forgery. They would conclude that an intelligent signal might be in the unusual spectral lines of the star.

Fifteen such stars, whose spectra, scientists have found, contain anomalous radiation, could be within a hundred light-years of the sun. No one can as yet satisfactorily explain why their signatures seem forged. *All of the stars are of types suitable for sustaining intelligent life.*

To a superbly attuned society such as the Perseans would have now become, the science of mind over matter might have been their final objective in both travel and communication. To physically transport individuals from galaxy to galaxy—which future generations of their race would wish to do—would have involved too vast a drain on energy, food, and other resources, as well as time.

They might, therefore, have been well advanced in a remarkable process that could have changed their whole conception of interstellar travel. One that could have overcome the seemingly insurmountable problem of sending individuals, even with their biologically extended life expectancies, on journeys lasting hundreds or thousands of years.

Their scientists might have been approaching a stage where living creatures like themselves—or any other material—could be transmitted through space as radiation traveling at the speed of light.

Already their laboratory tests might have successfully achieved these astounding transmissions with simple life cells by transforming the cells into a form of energy. After transmitting this energy from one point to the next, a further sophisticated process would reconvert the energy back into matter—in precisely the same form as it was before being originally transmitted.

Simultaneous research could have already been well advanced in a system by which the precise detail of each

196

of a body's components, and the exact manner in which each was constructed and arranged, would have been broken down and transformed into a code of signals. After being transmitted, the signals would produce a blueprint of the original body, from which a replica might be reconstructed from the same material or atom elements available at the new destination.

In the first method no trace of the original life form would remain at the point of transmission. In the second, it would still exist, together with a duplicate of it, faithfully reproduced in every delicate detail, at the receiving source.

By this bizarre technique the scientists of a superrace could consider selecting the elite of their society for extensive duplication. In other words, to actually mass-produce its finest physicists and astronomers, its most illustrious planners and mathematicians, and its most profound philosophers.

In this way the intellectual future of its creative race on an alien planet would be assured. They would be virtually certain that, whatever problems and conditions faced these interstellar pioneers, solutions would probably be found to surmount them.

They would realize, of course, that even the most minute miscalculation in the computerized dismembering of the atomic structure of a living being could produce the most horrific mental and physical mutilations during their reconstruction at the destination.

During the initial experiments complete body transplants by radiation would probably have resulted in years of controversy, on moral and ethical grounds. What would be the psychological effects on an individual who suddenly had to encounter and even exist alongside a "living photostat" whose mind, emotions, reactions, and memory entirely mirrored his own? In the cases of those selected for this kind of plasmic embarkation to another world, must their families be carbon copied with them? Weren't the monstrous permutations of faulty transmission too obvious to allow even contemplation of such an outrageous scheme?

On a desperate planet such as Perseus, there would no doubt have been countless other objections from every section of this highly sensitive society which had existed for so long without deformity and imperfection in its mental and physical makeup. But now faced with a crisis of such catastrophic magnitude—the terrifyingly simple question of survival—the Perseans would have been forced to abandon any objections based on ethics.

Here on Earth some eminent scientists already believe that this startling method of transporting man as radiation or by coding and decoding his atom elements might one day be realized. Quite obviously, from man's present sources of knowledge, energy, and technology, its operation is entirely out of the question. But how can it be ruled out for all time?

Throughout our history new and incomprehensible ideas have been scoffed at as "irresponsible rubbish" by those whose influence upon society should have led them to develop open minds. When the first steamships were made, one illustrious professor made this derogatory prophesy: "Men might as well expect to walk on the moon as cross the North Atlantic in one of those steamboats." How right he was!

There were innumerable "experts" around to laugh at George Stephenson's idea of railway engines; at Marconi's "idiotic" theories on sending radio signals; at the grotesque suggestion that carriages might actually move without horses.

When Orville Wright flew his first airplane some newspapers refused to publish "this ridiculous story." When Marconi spanned the Atlantic, even the great Thomas Edison said: "Impossible." And even President Eisenhower shrugged off man's first space object, *Sputnik I,* with the reported remark: "The Russians have put a small ball up in the air. That does not raise my apprehensions one iota."

So now, after men have trundled on the moon, orbited and landed instruments on the nearer planets, and even sent a probe on its way *out* of the solar system, how can we likewise scoff at the idea of creatures such as ourselves being reduced to radiation or energy for the kind of galactic journeys a threatened Earth may one day force us to take? It might, therefore, be wise to consider the idea further.

As explained earlier, a consequence of Einstein's Special Theory of Relativity would be that on a spaceship capable of traveling at the speed of light, all time-dependent events would appear to stop. Clocks would no longer function, passengers would enter a state of suspended animation, and all distances could be covered in zero time—or instantaneously.

In April 1970 the British Interplanetary Society's journal, *Spaceflight,* published a remarkable paper entitled "The Phenomenon of Time Dilation." D. F. Lawden, professor of mathematical physics at Britain's University of Aston, claimed the only way in which a spaceship and its crew could travel at the limiting velocity of light would be by first transforming both ship and crew into radiation.

"However," he goes on, "if we are prepared to contemplate such a possibility, the spaceship has become superfluous; since pure radiation requires no protection in space, neither does it require water, oxygen, and food!"

Because of the obvious threat to the radiated astronaut from any distortion of the beam during transit, Lawden suggests that "the proper solution to space travel at the speed of light is not the straightforward conversion of astronauts into radiation, but by impressing the pattern of the matter distributions within these men upon a beam of electromagnetic waves according to a suitable code of modulation. Reception of the signals at the arrival terminal could then be arranged to monitor the reconstruction of the astronauts from material available there."

Dealing with questions of personal identity, he writes: "It is reasonable to assume that the replicas of the astronauts constructed at the distant planet will behave in every way like their prototypes. Since the brain structures of the replicas are identical with the brain structures of the originals, the replicas will possess the same memories as the originals, including memory of recent events on Earth."

And what of a man's "soul"? What, you may ask, becomes of that? "I prefer to think of it as some kind of psychic field which is generated by the material of the brain and is entirely dependent upon the characteristic organization of this material for its continued existence," proclaims Lawden, and speculates on the possibility of transferring only the "mind" through the universe, without it accompanying the physical body—once the interstellar routes have been pioneered by using conventional modes of transport.

If all of this seems far too much like science fiction to even contemplate, consider for a moment the fact that the vast part of an atom is empty space. If its nucleus were the size of a tennis ball the electrons whizzing around it would be nearly a mile away. So, imagine what would happen if it were possible to completely remove the space so that the nucleus and the electrons were packed tightly together.

In the case of a human being—who is, of course, like everything else, constructed entirely of atoms—only a minute trace of physical matter would remain. Bones, tissues, and brain would disappear. When one considers, therefore, that man is almost entirely composed of space, theories like human radiation may not sound quite so preposterous.

All forms of communication available to twentieth-century man are, so far, restricted to physical laws and known dimensions. At the speed of radio transmission, direct useful interstellar two-way contact with distant stars, even in our own galaxy, is quite impractical.

So, is there some quite different method that need not conform to these normally accepted physical codes? Could, in fact, man one day be equipped to make mental contact with extraterrestrial beings? Are some super-races already using mind-to-mind communication as they travel across the universe?

A tremendous amount of serious investigation is going on all over the world into the exciting possibilities of using mental telepathy and extra-sensory perception (ESP) as a practical form of communication. Imagine the boundless ways in which this technique—once established—might be adapted in attempts to contact remote intelligences.

Suppose that—through some as-yet untapped power contained in the human mind itself—some form of thought wave that need not conform to the normal dimensions of time and matter could be attuned to transmit and receive messages from beyond our solar system. The years required for radio waves to span these incomprehensible distances might be reduced to a moment. For who knows the speed of thought?

At the International Astronautical Congress in Paris in 1963 it was proposed that telepathy might be used by moon explorers to keep in touch with each other and with base control on Earth.

In Russia a number of research centers are making extensive investigations into the use of thought transference. Their object is to bring it in line with known physical laws.

Remarkable and quite inexplicable things seem to occur in the nebulous haze of that strange world of the mind. American physicist Dr. E. Dewan of the Air Force Cambridge Research Laboratories in Massachusetts claimed he was able to control the Alpha rhythms of his mind to switch an electric light on and off.

Dr. Harold Puthoff, a quantum and laser physics specialist, and Russel Targ, a plasma and laser physicist, had been investigating phenomena such as telepathy and psychokinesis (the movement of objects without contact) since the middle of 1972. Then, in the spring of 1973, these two eminent physicists at Stanford Research Institute in Menlo Park, California, conducted some remarkable scientific experiments with a young Israeli, Uri Geller, who is reputed to be able to bend metal objects by mind-power, among other things.

The handsome, twenty-six-year-old Uri Geller was brought from Israel to America by Dr. Adrija Pulharich, a scientist and psychic-research investigator who wished to test Geller under strict scientific supervision.

Even before Puthoff and Targ's tests, several well-known scientists had witnessed some of Geller's talents. For instance, Professor Wernher von Braun found that an electronic calculator he had brought along refused to function normally in the young man's presence. Physicist Gerald Feinberg of Columbia University in New York had like millions of T.V. viewers since watched him bend metal objects without even touching them. And at the Max Planck Institute in Munich, Germany, Dr. Friedbert Karger claims he saw Geller stop cable cars, shatter rings, and change the shape of other objects.

The Stanford Research Institute experiments were rigidly controlled. Some of them were filmed and video-taped to check if some form of mass hypnosis might have been involved. Puthoff and Targ provided all the materials used, and even brought in an expert magician to watch for any sleight-of-hand maneuvers during the tests.

In one experiment, a precision balance, placed beneath a bell jar, was connected to a chart recorder. Without touching anything, Geller somehow caused the balance to respond—as though some kind of force had been applied to it. That force, registered by the chart recorder, was shown to be ten to a hundred times greater than could have been produced by striking the bell jar or the table, or jumping on the floor.

Further experiments showed that by moving his empty hand near a magnetometer—used for measuring magnetic fields—Geller caused a full-scale deflection. The scientists also witnessed Geller bend a steel band in a way that would normally have required more than a hundred pounds of applied pressure, but, as he actually touched the band on this occasion, the experiment was disqualified.

One series of tests involved shaking a numbered die inside a steel box. Eight times out of eight Geller predicted the correct number—a feat mathematically calculated at less than one chance in a million of being chosen randomly. In the same series, he correctly located on twelve consecutive occasions an object switched about between ten identical film cans.

Following these closely monitored tests, both scientists agreed that they had no scientific explanation. "All we can say at this point is that further investigation is clearly warranted," they announced.

The experiments claiming proof of some form of extra-sensory communication between dolphins are well known. It is believed that the dolphin uses its own natural sonar device for covering a wide range of sounds, some quite out of range of the human ear. Through a form of in-built stereo receiving mechanism, it can not only locate objects, but also tell their size and shape. For years scientists have been using sophisticated photoelectric devices to unravel the mysterious language of the dolphins—that fascinating series of high-pitched whistles, barks, grunts, and clicking noises they continually emit. Using an automatic food dispenser synchronized with the devices, they are encouraging dolphins to pronounce human words. And after all, talking to a dolphin might be very similar to decoding messages from some extra-terrestrial intelligence.

If super-races now use thought transference as the

only means of communication, have they long abandoned radio, lasers, and other means? If so, all their efforts could be wasted on us until we too are able to develop our own minds to such a delicately tuned state.

It is a simple matter for practical scientists to scoff at theory simply because the restricted laws with which they are familiar do not give them a logical conclusion. Man, as yet, can have no mathematical formula, no matter how complex, that can show how, for instance, a clear-thinking, highly intelligent individual can suddenly become a babbling idiot or a ruthless killer by some slight shift in his mental metabolism.

What must surely be accepted is that if ESP and mental telepathy are eventually controlled, the advantages to any race that possesses them would be immeasurable. For man, it might well open that Alice in Wonderland door to the unknown, the key to which, like Alice, we cannot quite reach. And once open, we might find a whole host of extraterrestrial societies waiting on our doorstep—societies who have for centuries been masters of their own minds.

TWELVE

THE LOST CIVILIZATIONS

Had it not been for natural catastrophes, our own civilization could well have flourished into a super-race by now, capable of reconstructing our solar system, of interstellar travel, and of widespread inter-galactic communication. Man's "brain" could now be orbiting in other distant solar systems in the form of computerized satellites.

It is believed that about thirty-four hundred years ago Crete and its tiny island neighbors in the sun-drenched Mediterranean were occupied by a remark-able race we now call the Minoans. They had built cities with magnificent palaces and luxurious, air-conditioned homes. They had developed an advanced form of writing and could produce exquisite works of art. They were able to navigate the oceans.

Suddenly this highly developed intelligent and sensi-tive civilization vanished from the face of Earth in the monumental violence of a gigantic volcanic eruption that buried them and their proud cities under a hundred feet of burning ash. A five-thousand-foot mountain on the beautiful island of Stronghyli belched its savagery with a terrifying fury that is now estimated to have been equal in intensity to several hundred hydrogen bombs.

And when this geological insanity subsided the whole center portion of Stronghyli sank into a gaping grave in the seabed. Those pieces that remained are now known as the Santorini islands.

To imagine the magnitude of this furious holocaust consider the records of the Krakato eruption in the East Indies in 1883. That one blasted a column of fiery dust thirty-three miles high, scattered rocks for fifty miles, and the fourteen-hundred-foot volcano collapsed into a six-hundred-foot sea crater, causing thirty-six thousand people and nearly three hundred towns to be destroyed in the tidal wave that followed. And that eruption, heard two thousand miles away, is believed to have been many times smaller than that of Stronghyli, where tidal waves could have towered a mile high.

But the effects of all this on the stage of man's technological and sociological evolution may well have been even more colossal. The intellectual blueprint for Western civilization as we now know it can be traced back to the cultures of ancient Greece. But at that time primitive Helladic tribes were the only inhabitants of Greece. It is believed that it was from the few scattered survivors of the stricken Minoan people— probably those who were away on sea voyages at the time of the catastrophe—that the Greeks developed their culture.

Those Minoan refugees, think some historians, could have fled to the security of the Greek mainland, which would have escaped the deadly volcanic fallout. There they would have taught the Greeks their sciences, their elegance, their mathematics, and their artistry.

They could also have shown them how to build their great temples and lofty palaces.

In 1967 scientists unearthed a Minoan town on the island of Thira—a portion of the shattered island that did not sink beneath the sea. Professor Angelos Galanopoulos of the Athens Seismological Institute, who had, ten years earlier, discovered human teeth among the ruins of a stone house at the base of a mine shaft on Thira, believes the dramatic story of Santorini could even be that of the legendary lost island of Atlantis. Plato's description of Atlantis could fit perfectly the size and features of Santorini, says Galanopoulos.

Some historians also believe that the cataclysm that virtually extinguished the Minoans could have caused the ten biblical plagues that swept Egypt, 450 miles away. Poisoned fish, blood-colored rain, and violent atmospheric disturbances might well have created these legendary horrors. The biblical dates of Exodus and the dates estimated for the destruction of Santorini are in remarkable agreement.

Now, let us suppose that by a slight twist of geographical fate the Santorini devastation had taken place a thousand miles away and did not, therefore, cause damage to Minoa. That nature had allowed the brilliance and vision of the Minoans to go on accumulating at an ever-increasing rate over the centuries. Imagine what profound effects the development of that intelligence would now be having on twentieth-century mankind. It might well have put us centuries ahead of our present stage in technological and sociological evolution. In fact, well into the glorious category of a super-race, able to master techniques far beyond our wildest dreams.

And how many other civilizations might have built their magnificent edifices of wisdom and understanding, only to have it all swept away in the merciless geological vandalism of our angry, restless planet thousands of years ago. If only we had not been forced to keep starting over and over again, man might even now be reaching for the stars.

How many scientists and philosophers may lie cremated beneath the ashes and debris of those long-dead rivers of hell? And how many of their ancestors could now be carrying their untold secrets far and wide among the outposts of space?

The ancient Greeks, for example, would probably have reached the present stage of Western technology within two hundred years—and certainly no more than five hundred—if their glorious empire had not fallen because of social and political instability all those centuries ago.

It is virtually certain that they would by now have had interstellar spaceships simply by the normal process of development of the remarkable scientific knowledge they possessed in those early days. For even then they had clocks and steam turbines, knew about atoms, had accurately measured the diameter of Earth and the distance of the moon, and had primitive knowledge of electricity (a word actually derived from the Greek).

But probably the most incredible evidence of Greek ingenuity was dragged from the seabed in 1901 . . . a precisely built computerlike device that could calculate the motions of stars and planets. This unusual piece of ancient mechanism—believed to date back to about 80 B.C.—now stands in the Greek National Archaeological Museum in Athens. Crumbling and corroded after those many centuries beneath the sea, its dials, gear wheels, and inscribed plates offer breathtaking clues to the scientific awareness of that remarkable race.

In 1958 Professor Derek J. de Solla Price, aided by a grant from the American Philosophical Society, visited Athens and made a minute examination of the fragments of this exciting device unknowingly found by a party of sponge divers working two hundred feet off the tiny southern Greek island of Antikythera. The

208

divers had brought up bronze and marble statues from the wreck of an ancient ship. Among what were first thought to be lumps of corroded bronze broken from one of these statues were found the fragments of what has now become known as the Antikythera mechanism.

In June 1959 *Scientific American* published de Solla Price's fascinating report of the research work into this shattering discovery. This is how he describes the original object: "Consisting of a box with dials on the outside and a very complex assembly of gear wheels mounted within, it must have resembled a well-made eighteenth-century clock. Doors, hinged to the box, served to protect the dials, and on all available surfaces of the box, doors, and dials there were long Greek inscriptions describing the operation and construction of the instrument."

How can we be sure that the device is so ancient and did not originate in more modern times? It is now accepted that the wreck took place during the first century B.C., proved by archaeological analysis of the pottery and other objects from the ship. Experts also confirm that the form of inscribed lettering on the clock's fragments also belongs to that period. One piece of inscription is from an astronomical calendar similar to one produced about 77 B.C.

The device seems to have been operated by an axle that came through the side of the casing which, when turned, manipulated gears so that different pointers moved at various speeds around the dials. One dial, at the front, has two scales, one of which is fixed and shows the months of the year. Both scales are marked off in degrees and this dial could show the annual motion of the sun in the zodiac and the main risings and settings of bright stars and constellations throughout the year. Some of the back dials seem to indicate the main lunar phases, while others are thought to give information on the planets Mercury, Venus, Mars, Jupiter, and Saturn, then known to the Greeks.

"The Antikythera mechanism," explains de Solla

Price, "is like a great astronomical clock without an escapement, or like a modern analogue computer which uses mechanical parts to save tedious calculation." There is no way of knowing whether it was turned automatically or by hand, but it might have been operated from a device such as a water clock.

Other clockwork computers similar to this Greek instrument appeared later in Islam, China, India, and during the European Middle Ages. In the Museum of the History of Science at Oxford, England, is a thirteenth-century Islamic geared calendar-computer whose dials show the various cycles of the sun and moon.

"It seems likely," says de Solla Price, "that the Antikythera tradition was part of a large corpus of knowledge that has since been lost to us but was known to the Arabs. It was developed and transmitted by them to medieval Europe, where it became the foundation for the whole range of subsequent invention in the field of clockwork." And he concludes: "The Antikythera mechanism was no flash in the pan, but was a part of an important current in Hellenistic civilization. It is a bit frightening to know that, just before the fall of their great civilization, the ancient Greeks had come so close to our age—not only in their thought, but also in their scientific technology."

It is incredible to think that today, so long after the scientific maturity of the ancient Greeks, and thirty-four hundred years after the extinction of an advanced society like that of the Minoans, there are still African tribes who regard the sun's eclipse as heralding the end of the world.

When scientists arrived to register the eclipse on June 30, 1973, the El Molo tribe on the shores of Lake Rudolf in Kenya were firmly convinced the equipment they brought with them was designed to take their sun away. They were just as apprehensive as were the ancient Babylonians and Chinese, who—despite the fact that their priests and astrologers could accurately calculate the dates when eclipses were due—still sacrificed animals, and even humans, to pacify the "devouring dragon"—shouting, praying, and banging gongs to drive it away. Of course, this always succeeded!

Eclipses of the sun run in a series known as the Saros (a period of a few days over eighteen years). Sir Fred Hoyle has shown how Stonehenge can be used to calculate the Saros simply by moving a series of black and white stones round the "Aubrey Posts"—rings of pillars whose outlines are still just visible. In other words, even long before the Antikythera mechanism, Stonehenge was probably the first giant "computer."

Oddly enough—despite the still-primitive fears and suspicions of the El Molo tribe in Kenya—it was in their territory, in a bed of silt and gravel alongside Lake Rudolf, that the skull of man's earliest known ancestor was found in October 1972. It seems strange that, in an area where man has been around the longest time, man's technology has not developed. The skull, discovered by British anthropologist Dr. Richard Leakey, was found by scientists at Cambridge University to be three million years old—which means we've been around two million years longer than we thought we had.

The skull, meticulously pieced together from about two hundred shattered remnants found by Leakey, appears to have contained a similar brain to what present-day man possesses. Could it be that a highly civilized community such as the Minoans' once existed around Lake Rudolf, only to have been wiped out by some ancient catastrophe, all traces of which the centuries have long since hidden beyond reach?

At the time of his remarkable discovery, Leakey is quoted as saying: "From thigh bone deposits, there is no reason to doubt this individual could walk. It is also reasonable to suppose he had some fairly sophisticated means of communication—possibly a language." Leakey's father, Louis, who died in 1972

211

after spending most of his life in the fascinating study of primitive man, had always believed that Africa was the "Garden of Eden" from which the earliest man originated and then moved into Europe, Asia, and the Middle East.

The discovery of curious and unexplained objects has been reported in magazines like *Scientific American* and *Nature,* as far back as the mid-nineteenth century. Electric batteries, manufactured many centuries ago and loosely labeled "ritual objects," have been found in a Baghdad museum.

Objects of this kind have been mentioned in many ancient references. And if they really *were* batteries, what were they for? Some writers suggest they were used for electroplating materials such as gold. This is unlikely. Gold can be applied far more easily in thin-leaf form. And, anyway, to electroplate gold requires very special chemicals and technique. Furthermore, the type of battery usually described could not deliver the required current before it "polarized," or ran out of power.

However, these copper-iron batteries, we consider, *could* have been used for telegraphic communication. Each would produce about one volt. A group of them providing a hundred volts could give enough energy to power a simple gold electroscope (a flapper arrangement something like a pair of inverted book pages). This would open and close as the hundred volts were switched on and off. And the apparatus could then operate over, say, a hundred miles.

If a single wire network had been set up between the temples of the priests and the palaces and government buildings of an ancient king, a communication link could have been used to pass messages in a simple code similar to Morse.

A single bare-wire telegraph system of this type was produced in the eighteenth century, fifty years before Samuel Morse devised his famous code. Such a system would not have been beyond the ingenuity

212

of the Greeks and ancient Middle East civilizations and might, possibly, explain such things as "prophecies" of the Oracle of Delphi.

THIRTEEN

HAVE THEY BEEN HERE BEFORE?

Abraham Lincoln was President of the United States, the world's scientists were immersed in Charles Darwin's outrageous theory of evolution as the humanists were demanding an end to slavery. In Russia, Tolstoy was engrossed in his epic *War and Peace* as the Americans tore at one another's throats in the anger of the Civil War.

But 113 light-years away from it all, the last remaining community of scientists and philosophers on the planet Perseus 2 might have been performing their one final duty before following the rest of their chosen race on journeys across the galaxy . . . that of setting up a long-life radio beacon on their abandoned make-shift planet. It would have been a powerful signaling unit, automatically operated from the increasing energy source of its dying sun, that would transmit at all known radio frequencies up to, perhaps, a distance of two light-years—signals that the spaceship crew of any other advanced technology would recognize as unmistakably artificial in origin. These signals could guide an alien ship to the abandoned planet. The transmitting equipment would have been stored in an inert, temperature-controlled atmosphere—a sealed chamber under the ground. Only the antenna would have been above the surface.

Alongside the Persean beacon might have been placed a massive, indestructible monument deeply engraved with symbols and binary numbers depicting life on their original world—telling, in cold, mathematical terms, the tragic story of their flight to temporary safety on their sister planet, and finally identifying and locating the star systems to which their people had eventually headed in order to create new and permanent societies.

Man has already used this system of symbols to identify himself by placing plaques onboard the spacecraft *Pioneer*s *10* and *11*. Should any extraterrestrial intelligence encounter these craft, they will find the designs shown in Figure 9. It depicts a naked man and woman, drawn to scale, superimposed over the outline of the spacecraft. At the base are the sun and nine planets with the *Pioneer*'s trajectory as it leaves the third planet, Earth, and swings past planet number five, Jupiter.

In the center of the design, the location of our sun is shown by the intersection point of signals from fourteen pulsars, and the binary symbols on each show the frequencies of the pulsars at the present time. A million years from now it will be possible to calculate from these the time the spacecraft were launched from Earth.

The plaque left by a civilization fleeing across the galaxy for a haven in which to perpetuate their species, technology, and culture -could never truly record the many tragedies that might have taken place on such desperate journeys. It could never tell the drama of

Figure 9

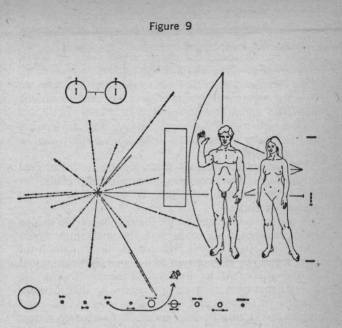

This plaque, sent out on board Pioneers 10 and 11, would tell an alien intelligence about Man and where he came from.

those who completed their missions and of the many who must have perished.

But the kind of plaque—part of which is envisaged in Figure 10—could still tell visitors a great deal. It would, in fact, be quite possible to tell those who found it the following story in the form of various symbols:

This is what we looked like and here is where we lived. Before the evolution of our sun made our world uninhabitable, eight billion of us lived on the first planet of our solar system. We developed space travel and half a million of us moved to the third planet of our sun. Here we built 150 starships of a type whose outline is shown on this plaque. We found fifty planets of other stars suitable for our form of life and three hundred thousand of us left to take refuge on them. We launched three ships to each planet and each ship carried two thousand passengers. In this way we hoped to preserve our race and our way of life.

We have also indicated where we went and how we launched our spaceships. If all else has failed, you who heard our signal and are now reading this plaque will at least know that we once existed and achieved a high technology. And you will know that many died so a few of us might live.

The complete plaque—probably made from gold alloy—might have contained many other details, for its size would not belimited, as were those on the *Pioneer* satellites.

Among the information on the section of the plaque shown in Figure 10 is the way the spaceships would have been launched and powered. A likely method for ships leaving a star system like Gamma Persei would be one advocated by Professor Freeman Dyson. He suggests that by maneuvering a vehicle so that it passes between two stars, such as those of the second component of Gamma Persei, one might find a free source of energy in the gravitational field that could create an enormous "slingshot" effect. And, due to the hydrogen-rich atmosphere in this "between" area, a ramjet would be "lit up" and start its journey with a good hard "kick in the pants"—all for free. This "Dyson dodge" is symbolized by the curly loop at the top of the plaque diagram, which also shows a funnel-shaped outline of a spaceship—the right design for a ramjet.

The rows of vertical and horizontal dashes on the right tell the number of ships launched, the passengers, and the total populations of both planets, all in terms of binary numbers. (The full details of these binary numbers and how the plaque can be "read" are given in Appendix 6.)

Because we obviously cannot visualize the shape of a Persean—or any other alien intelligence—we have drawn the form of a humanoid. The fifty lines looking

Figure 10

The Memorial Plaque on Perseus 2.

The three circles at the top describe the method the Perseans would have used to launch their spaceships. Below a figure represents the Persean race. Alongside are the two main planets, Perseus 1 and 2 (the larger of the five circles), with rows of

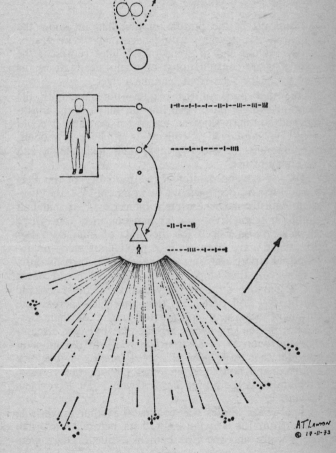

binary symbols showing the original population of Perseus 1, the lesser population of Perseus 2, who moved there.

Beneath is depicted the shape of an interstellar ramjet, how many were built, and the total number of passengers they carried. The fifty lines fanning out at the bottom show the destinations of the spaceships and, in some cases, the star constellations as they would appear from Perseus. (Fuller details in Appendix 6.)

like sunrays at the bottom of the diagram show the directions the starships would have taken. The groups of dots at the end of some of the lines represent the various star constellations of their destinations as they would be seen from Gamma Persei.

On other parts of the plaque—not shown on the diagram—might have been full star maps of the northern and southern skies as seen from Perseus. It could also have contained a collection of pictures, models, and diagrams of the Perseans, their technology, and their way of life.

To any advanced intelligence, the story of the Perseans' life and death would be apparent . . . the awesome catastrophe where eight billion died so that half a million might live—not as happens in a war where the *few* are sacrificed for the mass of humanity. For this would have been a different kind of war—an intellectual struggle against the invincible force of Nature.

However, that stark, lonely memorial could never tell a passing stranger how many of those cosmic "lifeboats" floundered as they struggled across the turbulent oceans of space. How many of their desperate passengers were wiped out by the disease-carrying bacteria of a strange new world the moment they set foot on it? But if only a fraction of the race survived and flourished on other planets, the sacrifice of billions of their predecessors would not have been in vain.

The United States was colonized by that brave little party from the *Mayflower*. Others before them—like the Vikings and the Elizabethans—failed. There were not enough of them. But several shiploads quickly followed the *Mayflower*, otherwise those first settlers could not have been successful.

Colonies of two thousand, such as the Perseans might have despatched, would, with sufficient resources have a good chance of survival on alien worlds.

The navigation data fed into the computers of that last interstellar Mayflower from Perseus 2 might well have been tabbed "Destination Earth." Its time of arrival? Perhaps 2000 A.D. And, should it one day sweep into our orbit, it could be far from the first such alien visit. For one of the most fascinating controversies of the century still captures the imagination of us all . . . *have* extraterrestrial intelligences visited us before?

Ever since the first flood of saucer-happy UFO-spotters began ringing up their local newspaper office in the 1940s, the question has pestered, intrigued, aggravated, and perplexed us.

Author Erich Von Daniken's screen version of his book *Chariot of the Gods* pulled in packed houses even in sober Moscow, though the Russian scientists seriously engaged in extraterrestrial research may regard some of his evidence of alien cultures on Earth much more cynically. The mysterious "bullet hole" Von Daniken mentions in the skull of an animal that died thousands of years ago (presumably in the days of bows and arrows and flint-headed axes) has since been shown to have been caused by a type of marine shellfish capable of boring regular-shaped holes of this kind, and the skull is now known to have been immersed in the sea at one period.

And yet what, scientifically, are the *chances* of aliens having visited Earth since it cooled into a stabilized planet four thousand million years ago? They are, it would seem, extremely high—possibly running into thousands of visits—though most of them would most likely have been made in the form of highly computerized artifacts either landing on Earth or orbiting it, such as one from a planet like Perseus might be doing at this moment.

There are good scientific reasons to assume the existence of at least one of these alien artifacts either here in Earth orbit or somewhere within our solar system . . . tiny, pulsating "worlds" that searches such as Anthony Lawton's may pinpoint out there in space.

Since our solar system was born some five thousand million years ago, our sun and its planets are estimated to have made twenty complete circuits of the galaxy. This means we must have strayed into the neighborhoods of countless other stars and their planets. And because each star has its own movement, its galactic neighbors are continually changing. A million years ago, the nearest stars to us would have been entirely different from those occupying such positions today.

Some idea of the immense variety of planets that could, throughout Earth's mobile history, have been within range of us and could, with sufficiently advanced travel and communication techniques, have paid us a call, is dramatically shown in G. V. Foster's recent paper, "Nonhuman Artifacts in the Solar System."

Within a distance of ten light-years of our sun are ten observable stars, some almost exactly like our own sun. But over long periods of time these stars are continually interchanging; as one moves out of that ten-light-year radius a new one moves into it.

It is estimated that in each million years forty-eight different stars will occupy that same radius, spending an average of 210,000 years there. This means that during the last four thousand million years, the planets of 192,000 different stars will have passed by us, less than ten light-years away. And some will have come quite close.

It has been calculated that once in roughly eleven million years a star passes within as little as one light-year—a mere interstellar "bus-stop" journey for a society advanced in space travel.

Now, if we extend that radius from ten to fifty light-years from the sun, the number of different stars passing within it over Earth's lifetime will have been 4,200,000. And within a 250-light-year zone the figure becomes a staggering 112 million stars spending an average time there of around five million years!

So, if only a fraction of those stars have advanced life on their planets, the number of possible visitors or automated messengers is still exceedingly great. And, says Foster, as our galaxy could be around thirteen thousand million years old, there is "every reason to suppose that large numbers of intelligent life forms were in existence before the formation of the sun's system."

Scientists' estimates of the total number of stars in the Milky Way capable of developing advanced technological civilization vary tremendously from two hundred thousand to ten thousand million. As the age of the galaxy is more than two and a half times that of our sun, Foster divides these figures by three. Even so, working on the lowest remaining estimate of sixty-seven thousand, he calculates the chance of a visitation from stars passing within ten light-years during the life of Earth to be just over one in eight.

On the higher estimate of 3,300 million stars, the chances work out at some sixty-five hundred alien visits.

"If," Foster says, "a compromise figure, say ten million, is selected as the best reasonable estimate of community proliferation, then the probability is that there have already occurred some twenty visitations."

By the same logic it can be reasoned that 108 visits have probably been made by aliens passing within a twenty-five-light-year radius of Earth; 420 in the fifty-light-year zone, and 11,200 visits by aliens able to cover 250 light-years.

The cynics will say, "All right then—where's the evidence?" Where are the remains of all those complex structures with the mechanics to collate our secrets into their memory banks and to perform the many tasks for which their extraterrestrial creators programmed them? Why haven't they left their "visiting cards" in the form of some recognizable souvenirs, plaques, or recording equipment?

The simple answer is that they probably have; we just haven't found them. Geophysical changes in the structure of Earth over many millions of years would have long since claimed all traces—buried them in the shifting sands, lost them in the turbulent interchanges of sea and land masses, decomposed them in the corroding atmosphere.

There could be one place in the world where the hidden past is still well preserved—the Antarctic continent. A huge land mass is concealed beneath the thick icecaps. It would not have been disturbed by earthquakes. In fact, this fresh-frozen slice of the past will eventually drift out of range of the Antarctic icebox, the top preserving layer will melt, and the land of a million years ago will reemerge. It is just possible that a nonhuman artifact might be found in the ancient flotsam left on the land surface.

A similar situation could apply to the tundra of northern Siberia, which has already revealed fresh-frozen animals, such as mammoths, and has caused much speculation on how this rapid freezing occurred.

However, these icy wastelands total less than five percent of Earth's surface, so the chances of finding an artifact there, though they might exist, are pretty slim. In any case, such a discovery will, of course, have to be left to our descendants.

Carl Sagan puts forward another interesting thought on the fate of alien artifacts in a letter to the magazine *Nature* in July 1973. In the summer of 1976 it is planned to land NASA *Viking* probes on Mars. After more than a year of careful study, four tentative sites have been chosen from still very limited photographic evidence.

Sagan, who helped in the selection, imagines what

would happen if an alien planet had chosen sites on Earth with the same planetocentric coordinates (latitude and longitude). He worked it out that three of their probes would come down in the ocean and probably sink without trace, and the other would land in Yellowstone National Park. In the latter case it *would* find life forms and possibly an intelligence of too inquisitive a nature—someone would probably dismantle the whole thing.

But assuming that many in the past have found safe and solid resting places, how do we know countless remnants have not been found by our distant ancestors? Would a caveman have the remotest idea what a TV antenna was for, except perhaps to sharpen one end and use as a spear? If, too, some of those early visitors had arrived in person, they would have found a world very different from the one we know today, a world as yet devoid of all but the simplest of organic life. The same race may even have returned subsequently, only to find it still in the same primeval stage. So why should they have bothered further when they would be surrounded by so many more livelier places to visit in the galaxy?

They may, of course, have selected other places in our solar system to deposit proof of their visits. On the moon, for instance, they might—undisturbed by man—have stood the test of time. It is unlikely, however, that we should find any on Mars, whose violent duststorms would rapidly bury anything smaller than a block of flats, and where they might be ground to fragments in a natural sandblast.

But, wherever they are, the discovery of these alien "relics" could be of far-reaching significance in our search for more of those elusive secrets of the universe. For even the simplest device of a super-race could well unravel a whole new field of astronautical technique that would cut short by decades our search for the stars.

What would these complex little messengers from the

stars be like? How would they operate? We can, of course, only guess, because it is quite beyond us to really envisage the highly sophisticated equipment of a society even a few hundred years in advance of our own, let alone perhaps a million years.

But, reasoning within our own technological range, the basic functions might be similar to those of NASA's two *Viking* probes planned to land on Mars in 1976 after taking nearly a year to travel the 440 million miles through space.

Much of the knowledge scientists hope to gain from the probes will be stored in intricate little memory units for transmission back to Earth. These plated-wire memories—which, like all other *Viking* components, will be heat-sterilized to avoid contaminating the "Red Planet"—will act as temporary storage points for data, except photography, from all the *Viking* studies. And the vital information they absorb might finally help to solve the centuries-old controversy . . . is there life on Mars?

In September 1973 the staff of NASA prepared a special report on *Project Viking* and what it is hoped to achieve. The following extracts from that report give a clearer idea of the great contributions probes of this kind can make in our exploration of space:

Each of the two *Viking* landers—looking like some gross mechanical housefly with its spindly legs and quivering antennae—will contain a miniature chemical laboratory which will automatically go through intensive analyses of the Martian surface and atmosphere for any possible signs of life. A ten-foot retractable claw will scoop up samples of the soil for inspection while other delicately attuned instruments check temperature, atmosphere conditions, and wind speed (*Viking* landers are designed to touch down in gales of up to 150 miles per hour).

If there is life on Mars, it is probably in the form of microorganisms. By three different types of experi-

226

ment in their minilaboratories, the *Vikings* will prove conclusively whether or not life exists.

Two facsimile cameras will take panoramic, color, and infrared pictures, and even exciting stereoscopic views of a complete 360-degree area around the lander. These pictures could identify any higher form of life that might be around, and also show the restless drama of the planet's swirling duststorms.

The most urgent task will be to find water. Water means life. Mars is known to have water vapor in its atmosphere, and the subsurface polar caps are believed to be made up partially of ice. Scientists now want to find regions that could contain liquid water, if only for short periods. A highly sensitive "diviner" will be able to detect even the tiniest of water traces.

Mars does not have the most hospitable of climates. It is dry and cold. But many scientists still believe life could exist there. If the *Viking* probes confirm this, we shall then know for certain that on planets with more inviting climates like our own, life must most definitely exist—and this could mean millions of them throughout the galaxy. And even if the inquisitive mechanical senses of *Viking* do not detect life on Mars now, they would tell us if it once did exist there, and this knowledge would be almost as exciting.

Even over the comparatively short interplanetary distance between Earth and Mars, a one-way radio message will take twenty minutes, so investigations by *Vikings* that cannot be interrupted by such long-delayed commands from base will be performed entirely automatically by preprogrammed computers.

And as the lander sections of the two *Vikings* continue with their painstaking experiments on the surface, the remaining sections, left in orbit overhead, will be observing duststorms, cloud formation, and variations in temperature and humidity.

High-resolution cameras will record more vital information on the overall characteristics of this mysterious world that has captured the fantasies of writers for centuries.

Operations like those to be performed by America's *Vikings* and the Russian *Mars Landers*—and, no doubt, much more advanced work as yet beyond man's ingenuity—may well have taken place many times in its history in alien space probes to Earth.

They would, however, need to house far more complex methods of storing and analyzing the evidence they found here because of the many years it would take for information to be fed back to their parent planets such vast distances away. If, for example, Archimedes's famous cry of "Eureka" had been put over a Milky Way radio network program direct from his bath, listeners on the far edge of the galaxy would be getting the good news around the year 79,730 A.D.

FOURTEEN

ARE *WE* ALIENS?

Are we *all* descendants from another world? Are our original ancestors still out there somewhere? Some scientists are convinced we began our evolution as microscopic life forms that, in some way, arrived on Earth from a distant planet thousands of millions of years ago.

But how? There are a number of theories. At around the turn of the century, a Swedish chemist, Svente Arrhenius, suggested that life first arrived here as bacterial spores which, after escaping from another world, were driven across the galaxy by the pressure of radiation from powerful stars. It sounds feasible, except that the intense radiation to which they would have been exposed would surely have exterminated them.

A further theory was that these primitive life forms "hitchhiked" a lift across the galaxy embedded in the oldest spaceships of all time—meteorites.

Although meteorites weighing up to two thousand pounds have been seen to fall, most are burned up to tiny, harmless grains by Earth's atmosphere. Yet so many reach us that it is estimated they increase the world's mass annually by five million tons. And many of these are found, from radioisotope analysis, to be as old as Earth.

In 1961 the meteorite theory caused one of the most impassioned scientific controversies of the century. The New York Academy of Sciences received an astonishing report. Three scientists had applied the very latest chemical analysis to samples of a famous meteorite that fell at Orgueil, France, in 1864, and claimed to have found "the first physical evidence of life forms beyond our planet."

They were paraffin hydrocarbons which, on Earth, are found only in living organisms. Wherever this meteorite came from, they said, something lived!

And a year later came the sensational announcement from one of the scientists, Dr. Bartholomew Nagy of New York University, who had done further research with his colleague Dr. George Claus, that they had found fossilized life forms in meteorites that could not be identified with any of those on Earth. World reaction was explosive. Was this at last the real proof of extraterrestrial life that man was so ardently seeking?

Many eminent scientists joined in the big controversy, until, in 1963, the strange little creatures from outer space were irrefutably identified as mere pollen grains picked up either during the meteorite's journey through our atmosphere or during the many years the samples had lain in museums.

So if, as some researchers still believe, life originated elsewhere than Earth, was it brought from some other part of the universe by artificial means—by an interstellar spaceship or orbiting mechanical satellite launched thousands of millions of years ago by a distant super-race wishing to implant its species on our planet?

This makes sense to many who do not believe Earth is old enough to have given life the time to produce the sophisticated form that it has, whereas many of the stars—even in our own galaxy—are more than three times the age of Earth. Races there could have progressed millions of years beyond the scope of our own technology.

Two of the world's most eminent molecular biologists, Francis Crick of Cambridge, England, and Leslie Orgel of the Salk Institute at San Diego, California, put forward, at a joint meeting of the American and Russian science academies in 1971, the exciting idea that aliens deliberately infected Earth with its first life.

In 1973 they produced a fascinating paper on the subject, which was published in the respected science journal *Icarus*. In it, Crick and Orgel visualized how an extraterrestrial intelligence might have succeeded in "infecting" our planet with their life, by describing how we ourselves might one day attempt to do the same thing on other worlds.

A spaceship with a payload of, say, a thousand kilograms of assorted microorganisms—each with a different, but quite simple, nutritional need—would be launched into the galaxy. It need not travel at excessively high speeds. Its time of arrival would not really matter. If the vehicle traveled at only sixty thousand miles per hour it would, over a million years, be within striking distance of several thousand stars. If it traveled at one-hundredth the speed of light, it could do the same journey in ten thousand years—a very brief time, astronomically speaking.

The spaceship would have to home on a star, slowing down as it approached so that it could safely deliver its living payload. The packages of microorganisms would need to be made up and dispersed in a manner that would ensure their survival as they entered a

231

planet's atmosphere at high speed. We should be technologically able to produce spacecraft suitable for this kind of project by the end of the century.

Adequately protected against radiation, the microorganisms would be made up into assorted packages for a wide distribution on the various planets. It has been calculated that such life forms could be preserved for a million years if suitably protected and maintained at temperatures close to absolute zero.

"We conclude," wrote Crick and Orgel, "that within the foreseeable future we could, if we wished, infect another planet and, hence, that it is not out of the question that our planet was infected."

But why should we particularly want to inflict life on some other strange and distant world, except as some boast of our technological skill? It could be that, faced with so many threats to our continued existence on Earth—self-induced or otherwise—we might hope to perpetuate it elsewhere.

The chemical composition of living organisms must, to some extent, reflect the chemical composition of the environment in which those organisms evolved. So, if we were able to find in Earth life forms chemical elements that are extremely rare on our planet, surely this would be powerful evidence that life did come from some different world altogether.

There is one such "alien" chemical element which is vital to the functioning of our biological systems— molybdenum. And this metal certainly isn't abundant on Earth, whose content level is a mere 0.02 percent. Chromium and nickel—relatively unimportant in biochemistry—are far more abundant (0.20 and 3.16 percent). Is it not, therefore, more logical that life here originated on the planet of a star with a rich molybdenum content rather than on our own? And there are many such stars.

One final intriguing implication of all this is that the intelligence responsible for sending its seeds of life to us might well have successfully bred them on other worlds. Somewhere in the galaxy could be not only our original alien creators, but also many other distant relatives. Perhaps one day we might be able to organize a family outing to pop out and visit them.

A. Agrest, a famous Soviet mathematician, has, in recent years, suggested that Sodom and Gomorrah were destroyed by a nuclear explosion by alien visitors who blew up their surplus nuclear fuel before returning to their own planet. He points out that in the Dead Sea Scrolls' account of the stricken cities, the inhabitants were warned to leave and not look back. Those who did, died or lost their sight. Wouldn't this be the kind of warning that might be given for a nuclear explosion?

Agrest also says the Baalbek terrace, a platform composed of gigantic slabs of stone in the Libyan desert, could be the remains of an alien visitor's rocket-launching pad.

Dr. Vyacheslav Zaitzev, a philologist at the Byelorussian Academy of Sciences, associates many other biblical happenings with extraterrestrial visits, and says we may be on the threshold of a "second coming" of intelligent beings from space who have visited us in the past. He even describes Jesus Christ as a "cosmonaut."

The Mahabharata—a long history of Indian religion, legend and folklore—was written several thousand years ago. It translates into more than twenty volumes. One particular section describes a battle between the legendary characters Aswatthaman and Pandava. Could the following extract be describing a form of nuclear warfare?

"The valiant Aswatthaman invoked the Agneya weapon incapable of being resisted by the very gods. . . . Meteors flashed down from the firmament. A thick gloom suddenly shrouded the [Pandava] host. All the points of the compass also were enveloped in that darkness. Inauspicious winds began to blow. The sun himself no longer gave any heat . . . clouds roared in the welkin, showering blood. . . . The very elements seemed to be perturbed. The sun seemed to turn. The universe, scorched with heat, seemed to be in a fever. The elephants and other creatures of the land, scorched by the energy of that weapon, ran in fright, breathing heavily and desirous of protection against that terrible force. The very waters heated, the creatures residing in that element became exceedingly uneasy and seemed to burn. . . . Burnt by the energy of Aswattraman's weapon, the forms of the slain could not be distinguished."

Author Maxwell Cade suggests that highly advanced visitors might conceivably have left information about themselves and their culture by superimposing it, in microform, onto rock crystals. American scientists have already had remarkable success with this method of microstorage.

Legend and folklore have been interpreted by many researchers as containing evidence of extraterrestrial visitations. The legends of many ancient tribes include stories of gods in fiery chariots descending from the sky and producing superior children before moving on—offspring who, in their turn, may have been responsible for the occasional strain of genius that, from time to time in our history, has produced men far in advance of their own generation. Men like Leonardo de Vinci, who in the fifteenth century was able to predict so many of our twentieth-century innovations. Men like Albert Einstein and Isaac Newton.

Could some alien ancestry account for the amazing knowledge of the human body evident in the ancient Chinese art of acupuncture seven thousand years ago? Only in recent times has this technique been adopted in Western countries where, less than a century ago, we were still using the crudest, most barbaric forms of surgery.

According to legend, acupuncture developed when it was noticed that shortly after being wounded by

234

arrows in battle, soldiers sometimes recovered from illnesses they had suffered for years. The Chinese noted which points of the body the arrows had pierced and which illnesses had been cured. They then began to pierce the skin at these vital points, at first using pointed wooden sticks or thorns and later bronze and iron needles. By around 3000 B.C. gold and silver needles were employed. Today they are of stainless steel and are used for many conditions ranging from lumbago to anxiety states.

The theory of acupuncture is that flowing through the body is a circulatory system of "vital energy"—similar to that of our blood. There are twenty-six main circuits, known as *meridians*, each associated with a different organ or body function. In disease, the energy flow is unbalanced.

By piercing the skin at certain points (there are eight hundred of them) that energy flow is stimulated or sedated and its balance restored. An experienced acupuncturist is said to be able to discern from the pulses hundreds of different tensions and forms of activity. From these, he knows which meridians need to be balanced and at which points of the body, and how deeply he should insert his needles.

It all seems a remarkably complicated medical technique to have originated from a few stray arrows so many centuries ago.

Drawings and doll-like figures found during archaeological research have been interpreted by some writers as representing astronauts who visited Earth in ancient times and who were regarded by local inhabitants as gods whose untold power demanded worship. But the "spaceman" appearance of many of these have far different origins. Often these fascinating figures are simply a form of ancient religious symbolism such as that which still survives today among the Hopi Indians of Navajo.

In fact, the drawings and objects depict not the material form itself, but its "spirit." Venus dolls, for instance, carved with large breasts and genitals, were merely symbols of fertility—not deformed creatures that actually existed.

The Hopi Indians live in compact villages, or *pueblos*, in houses made from firmly packed soil baked hard by the sun. They dwell mainly in northeastern Arizona and produce superb pottery, carpets, basketwork, and inlaid and overlaid silver jewelry which is in great demand.

The Hopi are also famous for their carved and colorful Kachina dolls, which represent the spirits of many things, all of which have a religious basis. Sev-

Figure 11

Hopi Indian Kachina Dolls. Each doll represents the spirits of the deities of trees, animals and folk heroes. Although some appear to be wearing pressure suits, breathing gear and even antennae, this is purely coincidental. Each one can be explained, as has been the example of the chief's daughter shown in figure 12.

eral of these beautiful little dolls are shown in Figure 11. Certainly, without knowing their real purpose, it is easy to associate them with astronauts wearing breathing gear, antennae, pressure suits, and headphones. But they're not.

The religion of the Hopi people strongly resembles that of the ancient Greeks. They have many gods and also believe that all animate things (plants and animals), as well as some inanimate objets, have spirits. And the Hopi always visualize these in human form. The Kachina dolls symbolize this. So do the medicine men when they don the masks and garments of the Kachina deity. As long as these are worn, the wearer is no longer a man, but the animated spirit of the Kachina.

The Hopi recognize some thirty to forty deities ranging from four major gods, through lesser gods, to their own heroes who have been given godly status. Here there is a close parallel with Greek and other polytheistic religions.

Most of the spirits depicted by medicine men are those of animals or folk heroes. For example, Figure 12 is a Kachina mask of H'e-e'-e, an ancient heroine. The Hopi villages were being attacked by an enemy as H'e-e'-e, the chief's daughter, was being groomed by her mother. With only part of her elaborate butterfly hairdo finished—and since there were no men available to defend her village—H'e-e'-e ran to the other villages and rounded up an army of braves. She led the counterattack and drove off the enemy.

As a result, the Kachina mask and costume is a mixture of man and woman because although H'e-e'-e had the body of a woman, she had the courage and the heart of a man. The mask is black with a beard, the hair is rolled up and pinned on one side but hangs loose on the other. The costume is a woman's dress and shawl, with wedding sash and red moccasins. To signify the girl's courage, the outfit is completed

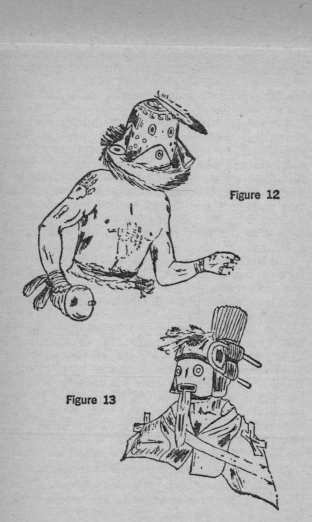

FIGURE 12. Hopi Indian mask of H'e–e'–e, the heroine daughter of an ancient chief. It is *not* a spaceman's mask.
FIGURE 13. Hopi Indian mask of Mastof. The dots on the mask represent the constellation Pleiades (on the right) and The Dipper (left).

with a bow and quiver full of arrows—the mark of a warrior.

This is the correct legend of H'e-e'-e, yet some writers would unhesitatingly interpret the mask as a space helmet and the rolled-up hairdo as the snorkel-type breathing gear of an astronaut.

The main color of the Kachina signifies its origin. For example, white is for east or northeast; red is south or southeast; yellow is north or northwest; blue or green is west or southwest. Black indicates directly downward (the Nadir). Patches of all the colors refer directly to the zenith, or upward.

Some of the Kachina costumes have star patterns. Mastof (a bear) carries the constellations of the Pleiades (Seven Sisters) on one cheek and the Big Dipper (Great Bear) on the other, as in Figure 13.

But they are still nothing more than the humanized form of the spirits of objects they worship.

One man who is convinced that aliens have visited Earth is one of the few humans to have actually ventured into space—Gordon Cooper, the American astronaut who piloted *Mercury 9* on its twenty-two-orbit flight in 1963. Forty-six-year-old Cooper, who now lives close by the very launch pad at Cape Kennedy in Florida, from where he was blasted into space, said, in a 1973 issue of the *National Enquirer:* "I think intelligent, extraterrestrial life has visited Earth in ages past. And I think there is a very real probability of Earth people resettling in other worlds, because eventually we are going to run out of land here. We are either going to have to find new worlds—and there are thousands of potential planets which have the atmosphere and temperatures we need—or drastically limit birth rates. If we do not, we're going to populate ourselves out of a place to live."

Cooper, who is now studying archaeology, was with an expedition team in South America which, he says, encountered the remains of a five-thousand-year-old civilization. He says that evidence they found there in-

239

dicated that the civilization was quite advanced and that its symbols and carvings were similar to those of cultures thousands of miles and an ocean apart.

"Even in those days," he says, "people were somehow traveling back and forth around the world. However, navigational instruments were not available to them. And their boats, from what we know of them, were not capable of crossing the oceans.

"That leads me to conclude that we had extraterrestrial navigators moving freely around the world."

The first clear evidence that this might have been the case is given by Professor Charles Hapgood in his book *Maps of the Ancient Sea Kings*.

Hapgood closely studied the original charts used by medieval navigators and found them to be of two types. One, for local sailing, simply showed coasts and rocks. But the others, though crudely drawn, showed continental outlines that could not possibly have been known to sailors of that period. For example, Antarctica appeared on one of the maps.

Hapgood therefore concluded that the maps were copies of ones produced many centuries before. If they were, it would have required an intelligence with considerable navigational skill to produce such accurate outlines of Earth's continents as they then were. Could they even have been reproduced from aerial pictures taken from a spaceship?

However, one must bear in mind that even with the crudest and most unwieldy vessels and navigational aids, sheer guts, sweat, and toil of past civilizations have accomplished what today would seem to have been impossible. It would be a simple matter for astronaut Gordon Cooper to explain away such gargantuan monuments as the pyramids by attributing them to some extraterrestrial visitor instead of the less-romantic conclusion that millions of mortals slavishly devoted many centuries of back-crushing labor in patient and remorseless dedication to their pagan leaders.

One has only to consider the remarkable personal saga of seven men in a flimsy boat who took on the violence of an ocean. Thor Heyerdahl had noted the close similarity of the reed boats used by South American Indians and the drawings of those found in ancient Egyptian paintings and rock carvings. He was also intrigued by the resemblance of the pyramids found in both these countries. He found a total of sixty such parallels between Egypt and South America.

Heyerdahl then conceived the bold plan of building an identical reed boat of Egyptian papyrus and actually sailing this vulnerable little craft across the Atlantic to South America. This really was doing things the hard way. As is dramatically documented in his book *Ra*, Heyerdahl's first boat (*Ra 1*) sank in the mid-Atlantic, but his second (*Ra 2*), sailed those tortuous 3,300-odd miles and reached its destination—water-logged but still seaworthy—fifty-seven days after leaving Safi in Morocco.

The Egyptians, of course, were skilled navigators and they could have known about, and used, polarized rock crystal as a natural "compass." This rock crystal can pick up stray sunlight, which changes the stone's color when it is pointed in a certain direction. So as long as the navigator kept his boat on a course that maintained the correct color glow in the stone, he was pretty sure to be heading roughly the right way. This ingenious little direction finder might not "beam in" on the hundred-yard landfall of a jetliner, but you'd certainly hit something as big as South America sooner or later.

If Heyerdahl could make that seemingly impossible journey, it is quite feasible that, allowing for fatalities on the way, large numbers of Egyptians could have done so in the past. They may well have set up a colony in South America that handed on to the resident natives the traditional arts of reed-boat making and pyramid building.

A rock crystal which may have been used by the

241

Egyptian navigator is cordierite (sometimes called *iolite*), a substance that looks like a piece of coal until you hold it up to the sky and peer through it. It then becomes a transparent browny-yellow. If you then point it toward the sun (even in overcast conditions) and rotate it slowly, you will suddenly see it flash blue—or a brilliant bluey-purple in the best stones. As you turn it further, the blue color goes.

What is happening is that the crystal is responding to the polarized light of the sky exactly as polarized sunglasses do. When the plane of polarization points at the sun, the stone is transparent. When it is at right angles to the sun, it turns blue.

These crystal stones are now very rare. Even a mediocre specimen would cost about three pounds (seven dollars and twenty cents) per ounce. And they are found in Norway, Iceland, Greenland, Finland, India, Africa, and Mongolia—all places renowned for civilizations of great travelers and sea voyagers of the ancient world.

The Norsemen, who recorded many of their sea sagas, tell of King Olaf II (995–1030 A.D.), referring to "a magic stone" that could find the sun even in cloudy or stormy weather. This was cordierite.

The Greeks too probably possessed cordierite. Possibly they used it in conjunction with their remarkable Antilythera mechanism, described earlier. This could have transformed it into the world's first automatic computer.

In his book *We the Navigators*, Dr. David Lewis of the Australian National University of Canberra talks about the amazing sea journeys of Polynesian navigators who accurately maneuvered their ships two thousand miles or more between islands in the Pacific. All archaeological evidence clearly shows that even the most distant parts of the ocean were colonized fifteen hundred years ago.

The Polynesians knew the constellations of the stars and their positions in relation to certain islands.

Other navigation aids were sea colors over reefs, cloud formations over islands, a knowledge of bird types and behavior, and even the reflection and refraction patterns of wind effects on the waves.

Dr. Lewis has actually retraced those incredible ancient voyages with experienced navigators from the Caroline Islands. He mentions that on one expedition the famous Captain Cook had onboard a Tahitian named Tupaia who, apart from being the island chief, was also a navigator priest. Cook was astounded at the detailed knowledge Tupaia had—without charts or instruments—of a vast area of the Pacific spanning roughly the size of the Atlantic from the U.S. eastern seaboard to the west coast of Africa. During a voyage to Hawaii, more than two thousand miles away, Tupaia *always* knew the direction in which his home island, Tahiti, lay.

But, though many more of these wondrous achievements of the ancient world may yet be explained in solid, down-to-earth terms, buried in a thousand of nature's hidden tombs may still be the undeniable evidence of some alien visitor.

Dr. Conley Powell, postdoctoral fellow in the Mechanical Engineering department of the University of Kentucky, wrote in a scientific paper published in 1972: "We must suppose that the solar system has been colonized in the past, perhaps many times and, perhaps, by many species. No evidence of such colonization has ever been found on Earth, but this is not surprising. Archaeologists are only too aware that our knowledge of many important human civilizations of only a few thousand years ago is sadly limited.

"In 1500 B.C. the Hittite Empire held most of Asia Minor, but, until late in the nineteenth century, we were unaware of its very existence. If our civilization were to collapse tomorrow, what would remain after a hundred million years? And that is only one-fiftieth of the age of the solar system."

Dr. Powell adds that, though there is conclusive

evidence that man himself originated on Earth, we are not sufficiently knowledgeable to rule out the possibility that species of animals, insects, or plants, brought here by alien colonists, still exist unrecognized.

FIFTEEN

THE MYSTERY OF THE DISCS.

Actual documentary evidence of aliens visiting Earth thousands of years ago could be hidden in the closely guarded archives of Peking Academy—evidence of such a startling nature that the Chinese authorities may be deliberately withholding publication.

Reports leaked from China could turn out to be the archaeological discovery of the century. Some seven hundred extraordinary granite discs found, in 1938, in caves in the mountains of Payenk Ara Ulaa, a region roughly the size of Korea, bear engraved symbols. One small excerpt of those many thousands of symbols tells of creatures "landing their craft" and meeting the local tribes.

With these mysterious discs—which were grooved like a gramophone record—were rows of graves containing the skeletons of unusual beings with particularly lightweight bone structures. Were these visitors from another planet? And if they were, could their thin, spindly frames indicate that they came from a small, low-gravity world? Or could they even have been specially bred as lightweight astronauts for interstellar travel?

Through direct but unofficial sources that Anthony Lawton has traced in Peking, we are now able to piece together something of this bizarre story contained in the few deciphered symbols published so far, and from written local legend.

The forbidding region of Payenk Ara Ulaa, or Payenk Ara Shaan, is known by a variety of names, including the popular but incorrect one, Bayan Kara Ula. It is in the old Chinese province of Tsing-Hai, now part of the People's Republic of China. It is not on the Tibetan border, as located in some other books and references. The particular spot involved in the incredible story we shall analyze is bounded by longitude ninety-six to ninety-nine degrees east and latitude thirty-three to thirty-five degrees north.

The area covers the valleys of the River Yalung and the River Tatung-Ho. The mountains here, Minyakonka and Jara, tower to twenty-five thousand feet, but the valleys—at only six thousand feet—can be pleasant and warm. As such, they have been inhabited by man since prehistoric times and it is thought from several archaeological expeditions that the area was much warmer about twenty thousand years ago.

It was during one of these expeditions, in 1937–38, that the Chinese archaeologist Chi Pu Tei and his assistants came across the discs and graves. The following is the only skimpy information on the expedition itself so far officially released from China, with our own remarks in brackets.

On the walls of "not many" caves, they found the sun and the moon painted on a background of star formations. [The term "not many" probably indicates between one and five.] During excavation of the caves for remains of the inhabitants, they found a number of skeletons with an average height of 1.75

246

meters [five feet six inches], which they believed might be from an extinct species of ape or gorilla, with a very fine-boned structure [i.e. slender but very strong, similar to the bones of birds or flying mammals]. Some references have incorrectly translated this to mean diseased or fragile bones. The stone discs they found were 0.8 meters in diameter and two centimeters thick [two feet six inches by one inch.] Each disc had a double-spiral groove on which were engraved symbols. When tested, these discs were found to be granite with a "high resonant frequency." [This term is confusing, but some later researchers claim they behave as if they carry electrical charges.]

In 1962 Professor Tsum Um Nui of the Peking Academy of Prehistoric Research—after many unsuccessful attempts by others over the years—announced that he had deciphered some of the symbols from one of the discs. Piecing these together with local legend, he produced an account of the intriguing events, a summary of which was given in the German publication *Das Vegetarische Universe.*

Tsum Um Nui states: "About twelve thousand years ago a group of things which were very ugly [local legend and literal interpretation] landed their craft because of . . ." [deciphered from the discs with no reason for landing given]. "They were hunted by the local people and hid in caves. Later, the local people returned with gifts, making signs of peace" [from the discs]. But, "When they emerged from the caves they were immediately killed because they were so ugly" [local legend].

No further details of the discs were revealed then, nor have they been since. But other Chinese legend tells of "little yellow creatures descending from the clouds with big heads and small bodies—so ugly that the local inhabitants attacked them." One ancient writing describes their grief at the loss of their spaceship during a dangerous landing in high mountains and of failure in their attempts to repair it.

247

Now, however, we can speculate more deeply on the whole baffling story of Payenk Ara Ulaa.

Many of the documents concerning the discovery could have been destroyed during the Chinese Red Revolution. Some of the material could well have been considered subversive and opposed to communist doctrine. If they still exist, they could, for similar reasons, have been deliberately suppressed.

But, let us first consider those strange discs scientifically. They are reported to be made from "granite with a high cobalt content." Granite is a basalt rock largely composed of silicates. Cobalt is a metal with magnetic properties and is rustproof. It will virtually last for ever.

Alloys of silicon, cobalt, and aluminum embedded in the spiral grooves of the discs could form a magnetic recording medium, similar to our magnetic tape-recorders, except that the information is "written" on the grooves. That information might even be induced to produce sounds which could be in the language of its original authors.

Alternatively, the discs could contain two "recordings." The top one might be the symbolic code crudely deciphered by Tsum Um Nui. A deeper one, embedded in the cobalt-loaded grooves, could be the magnetic recording still awaiting discovery.

This second recording might have been intended as a way of storing their information for thousands of years either for future visitors from their planet or for man's edification once he became sufficiently advanced to understand it. It might even contain a mathematical "language" with a binary code or a picture-forming code such as those for the star maps for extraterrestrial satellites as described in Chapter 7.

This double system of an easy-to-follow code of visible symbols and another more subtle one in the form of a "sound recording" could be precisely the sort a technically advanced race would use.

If we assume the characters read by Tsum Um Nui

were, say 0.5 centimeters square, each disc of 0.8 meters would have a total groove length of 100 meters, with twenty thousand characters on it. And if there were seven hundred discs, this would give a staggering total of fourteen million characters—equivalent to those contained in two copies of the Bible.

The binary magnetic coding could carry two hundred million "bits" of information! So why have only so few of those deciphered by Tsum Um Nui been published? Is the rest too controversial? Is it just too technical to understand? Some researchers claim the Peking Academy tried to forbid Tsum Um Nui from publishing any of it.

Now, what could be the significance of those painted star formations on the cave walls? By checking them against present-day formations and noting how certain star positions had changed, astronomers could quite easily work out the year in which the paintings were produced.

The positions of the sun and moon (also shown in the paintings) in relation to the stars would reveal the month and the day of that year. So they could literally state, for example, that whatever took place, happened "on the twenty-first day of the eighth month of the year 12,000 B.C."—just as a lecturer at a planetarium does as he moves his various star models backward in time. The paintings also show small open circles among the stars—all converging on Earth. Could they symbolize spaceships landing here?

But what really *did* happen in those forbidding mountains of Payenk Ara Ulaa? There are so many questions that cannot yet be answered outside of China.

Did a spaceship land? If so, was it done deliberately; did it crash or did some accident or mechanical failure force it to come down? If it landed, was it repaired and relaunched, or is it still deeply buried somewhere?

Were the local tribesmen so frightened of those

249

"very ugly things" that they killed and buried them? Or did the visitors bury their own dead before leaving Earth? Does there lie buried somewhere some recording machinery or type of phonograph for the discs? And would members of a civilization sufficiently advanced to undertake interstellar travel use such a cumbersome method of leaving records anyway?

Could those strange, lightweight skeletons be simply some form of ape with, perhaps, bones diseased by rickets—or could they even belong to the mysterious Yeti creature that has caused so much scientific controversy? The type of bone structure makes the latter unlikely. And apes don't bury their dead.

If we assume a spaceship *did* land intentionally, we could then indulge in a little bit of speculation. A survey party of the aliens might have set up a base in the caves to study the area and its isolated emerging community of humans, and record their findings while the rest of their colleagues stayed on the ship. They could have reckoned on few local inhabitants being around to threaten them in such a remote spot.

They would have had to remain for some time to produce those seven hundred discs. To find and prepare the granite, set up the cutting implements, and groove the recordings would have taken years.

Soon after this they may have inadvertently announced themselves to the local tribesmen and been attacked. They would then bury their dead together with evidence of their visit, and return to their own planet. No doubt the suspicious natives would place a "taboo" on the caves, so the graves and discs could have remained unmolested until their discovery in 1938.

One final question: If there has been an alien visit, where were they from? A slender, spindly creature would be best suited to a planet smaller than Earth but larger than Mars—and from somewhere outside our solar system. Somewhere with oxygen and a diameter of about sixty-five hundred miles. Perhaps, even, from the planet of Perseus! And the thin atmosphere of Tibet might suit the Perseans very well.

We believe Peking might well have the full story together with one or more of the original discs. Photographs would surely have been taken of the caves during the 1938 expedition, but none have been seen in the West.

Some reports claim that the discs are now in Moscow. This seems most unlikely. Each would weigh nearly three-quarters of a hundredweight—a total of nearly thirty tons. It would be a difficult enough task to get them from Payenk Ara Ulaa to Peking, let alone ship them four thousand miles to Moscow. And anyway, why *should* the Chinese go to the trouble of cleaning them all up to hand over to a nation with whom diplomatic relations have always been erratic?

The most logical reasoning is that only one, or possibly two, discs went to Peking and that the rest stayed at Payenk Ara Ulaa. And we can support this reasoning with further evidence on this desolate territory, its lonely people, and their strange behavior even to this day.

Dr. Andre Migot, archaeologist, anthropologist, physician, and Arctic explorer, who was probably the last Western scientist to travel through the Sino-Tibet mountains, describes it all in startling detail in his book *Tibetan Marches*.

Dr. Migot journeyed two thousand miles—at least half of them on foot—through the valleys of the Tatung-Ho, Yalung, and Mekong rivers (the Mekong river of Vietnam notoriety rises in the mountains of Payenk Ara Ulaa). Dr. Migot was commissioned by the Ecole Francoise d' Extreme-Orient in Hanoi to research archaeological and other aspects of the Buddhist religion.

During his remarkable journey he became very close to the Tibetans and fluently speaks and writes their language. He was awarded the Croix de Guerre

251

in military service—proof of the courage and determination needed for his grueling foot-slog through this forbidding land.

Dr. Migot found that the average Tibetan caravan is composed of between twenty and fifty ponies, mules, or yaks. In the rarified atmosphere of the high mountains, these beasts can only carry 120 pounds—less than the weight of two of those granite discs. To transport seven hundred of them the thousand miles to the nearest road at Chengtu would have taken four hundred animals, if one includes all the gear needed. A caravan of that size would have been strictly reserved for VIPs and government or military officials. No archaeologist could possibly have been permitted to use that incredible number of beasts, especially in the violently hostile atmosphere of superstitious people who hate tomb robbers.

Even if the authorities *had* given their consent, it would have been a virtually impossible undertaking. In 1946 the Ngo-log tribes, who inhabit the area, attacked a party of French explorers, killing three of them.

All of this tends to support the theory that if these discs exist, they are still in the caves where they are said to have been discovered in 1938.

From Dr. Migot's description of the Tibetan people in this area, they certainly do not fit the small skeletons found in those caves. He writes: "Against a background of small Chinese traders . . . your eye cannot help being caught by these handsome, gentle giants. . . . They move slowly through the crowd, dwarfing it —their massive, muscular frames lounging along with an effortless gait."

Dr. Migot also reports an uncanny experience as he was approaching the plateau of Tahoba: "Dawn was breaking, and in the uncertain light I stopped at the mouth of a little gorge to savor the silence and the peace of those great wastelands. Suddenly both were shattered by strange noises which seemed to come out of the shadowy recesses of the gorge.

"They were nothing like I had ever heard before—groans, strangled shrieks, wails of agony. These cries were certainly not made by the wind, nor by animals, nor—least of all—by human beings. It was impossible to attribute them to any natural cause and my blood froze as I listened to them.

"My pony was terrified too. He stopped grazing, pricked up his ears, and pawed the ground. I had dismounted, and if I had not kept hold of his reins he would have bolted. All at once the ghastly sounds ceased and all was quiet. The mystery is still with me today as part of a whole gamut of strange experiences undergone in a land where things happen that happen nowhere else on Earth."

Dare one wonder . . . is it *just* conceivable that a party of aliens are still there, watching us from their lonely outpost that few men of science could ever reach? Less than a dozen Europeans have penetrated this foresaken wilderness, and three of them were massacred.

If modern satellites could thoroughly "sky-spy" the area, infrared photography (sensitive to heat) might yet reveal some very strange traces—in the form of heat anomolies—that could be the signs of civilization. And, perhaps, if enough people keep asking enough questions, China will one day tell the world the full story of Payenk Ara Ulaa and clear up this fascinating mystery one way or the other.

But whether aliens have been here or not, man's search for his extraterrestrial counterparts will go on. During the next decade, "Operation Lifescan" will be intensified in countries all over the world.

More and more dedicated scientists will be sweeping more and more powerful detectors across the heavens, urging their searching radio antennae to probe deeper and deeper into the galaxy—determined to prove, once and for all, that the universe is not a barren graveyard of sterility, but a flourishing fraternity of sensitive and intelligent life of which we *must* one day be useful and acceptable members.

Early failures to contact other searching minds beyond our solar system will not deter this insistent new breed of space explorers. They will be patient. They will fully accept that—short of some unexpected stroke of luck—to achieve the most far-reaching goal in the history of the human race is going to be a slow, arduous, and, at times, heartbreakingly disappointing task.

There will be many setbacks, many false alarms, and many frustrations. There will be times when they will feel like taking a sledgehammer to stubborn instruments that remain deaf to someone they know *must* be out there somewhere. And even if, in eventual disillusionment, some drop out of "Operation Lifescan," there will be other fresh and eager minds ready to replace them. Man will not now abandon this enthralling mission.

The planet seekers of a dead world like Perseus could already have their navigation sights lined up on Earth. The advance message of their computerized "brain" orbiting our globe could now be pulsating more and more urgently.

And if someone *is* out there we *must* find them.

For even now, as mankind takes its first childlike steps into the threshold of a vast new unknown, what do we really know of the inscrutability of life and death? A million scientific equations may tell us that evolution has always been inevitable. That a cell will multiply into a man; that a life form in water will shape itself to swim; that a creature destined for the sky will somehow find its wings.

But how did it *really* all begin? And how does it all end? From where came those original ingredients—the hydrogen, the carbon, and the rest—to form these worlds without end? To produce an arm to reach out, a heart to break, a body to love and be loved, and a mind to ask and keep on asking. What is love? What is hate? What is death?

We never get quite close enough to arrive at the answers. Perhaps, one day, someone out there where we're heading will help us to find them.

APPENDIX ONE

Technical Details of Gamma Persei

Gamma Persei is a fairly bright star (magnitude 3.0) situated near the top of the circumpolar constellation Perseus, which is just above the famous Pleiades (Seven Sisters). Perseus is best seen near the zenith in November, December, and January at about 17.00 to 23.00 hours Greenwich Mean Time, or 22.00 to 04.00 hours Eastern U.S. Time.

Gamma Persei is directly above and to the right of Alpha Perseus, and both Alpha and Gamma are almost directly above Beta Perseus—better known as Algol or the Demon Star because of its constantly changing brightness.

When seen through a telescope, Gamma Persei is a brilliant golden-yellow major star with a sparkling, electric blue-green minor star companion which is itself composed of two stars very close together. This companion is a spectroscopic binary and this type of star is very unlikely to have a planetary system.

For amateur astronomers, the following are telescopic settings (Epoch 1970): right ascension—03 hours 02.6 mins; declination— + 53 deg. 23 mins, which makes the system visible from all areas of the United States. The major component is a GO 111-type yellow giant which has started to depart from the Main Sequence where it had probably been an F5 or F8 dwarf and, as such, was probably accompanied by planets—one of which was suited to sustain life.

The minor component is an A3 binary which is still on the Main Sequence.

Planetary System Dimensions

Having firmly identified the star as Gamma Persei, we can check a great deal of information by independent means. For instance, the two components of the system are separated by 2 arc secs. angle as measured from Earth. Using this angle, and knowing the parallax angle (0.011 arc secs.) we can calculate the actual distance separating the two stars.

It is: $\dfrac{2}{0.011}$ A.U. ie. 182 A.U. or about 18,000 million miles.

This distance of 182 A.U. corresponds to 100 "vertical steps" on sequence 2 (see Figure 7, Chapter 7) and the echo returns clearly show the nature of the two stars. There is a scaling in the echo returns for the planets, and if we look at the larger planetary dots—which we assume to be Perseus 1 and Perseus 2—we get a scaling of $\dfrac{1}{100}$ of 182 A.U. ie. 1.82 A.U. distance from its sun for Perseus 1 and $\dfrac{3}{100}$ x 1.82 A.U. ie. 5.46 A.U. from its sun for Perseus 2.

Their orbits correspond closely to Bode's law, and if we work through the calculations for possible orbits, these figures agree with Gamma Perseus A once being an F5–F8 dwarf Main Sequence star.

Possible Orbits for Perseus 1 and Perseus 2

If we assume that Gamma Perseus A has a mass of 1.1 times that of the sun, it is then 3.65 times as bright, and the first inhabitable planet (Perseus 1) will be at $\sqrt{3.65}$ or 1.9 times farther away than we are from our own sun, ie. at 1.9 A.U. The "year" of Perseus 1 is, therefore, $\sqrt{1.9^3}$, or 2.6 Earth years, ie. 950 of our days. The graphed position of Perseus 1 agrees with this.

Perseus 2 is the next planet but one and, according to Bodes law, it should be 5.12 times the distance of Earth from the sun, ie. 5.12 A.U. The year of Perseus 2 is, therefore, $\sqrt{5.12^3}$, or 11.8 Earth years, ie. 4,043 of our days. In fact it is "graphed" at 5.4 A.U., which would correspond to 13 Earth years—a very close agreement.

Since the "sun" Perseus A is so much brighter than ours, Perseus 2 could be a planet similar to Mars in terms of temperature and atmosphere. At that distance it is unlikely to be a gas giant such as Jupiter—although astronomically informed readers will note that it has an orbit similar to that of Jupiter.

THE LEGEND OF PERSEUS

Perseus is involved in one of the most romantic of the Greek legends associated with the stars. It tells how, returning through the skies from the conquest of the Gorgon Medusa, he finds Andromeda chained to a rock and about to be devoured by a sea monster. Perseus changes the monster into stone by holding up before it the Gorgon's head.

He then rescues Andromeda and takes her as his wife. After his death, goes on the legend, Perseus is transformed into a constellation. This depicts him in the heavens, his sword held high and holding Medusa's severed head.

APPENDIX TWO

STARS WITH SMALL OR UNSEEN COMPANIONS

Star	Light Yrs. Distance	Mass Sun—1
Proxima Centauri	4.3	0.0018
Barnard's		0.0011
Star	6.0	0.0008
Lalande 21185A	8.1	0.01
61 Cygni	10.8	0.008
BD + 5° 1668	12.2	—
Kruger 60A	12.8	0.009
Ross 614	13.1	0.08
AOe 17415-6	15.7	0.026
BD + 20° 2465	16.1	0.01
70 Ophiuchi	16.7	0.01

BD + 43°

4305	16.9	—
Eta Cass. A	18.0	0.01
Cin 2347	—	0.02
Cin 2354	—	0.02
Cin 1299	—	0.14
Alpha Ophiuchi	—	—
Mu Cass.	—	—

APPENDIX THREE

THE CRAWFORD AND VAN DER POL LDE. THEORIES

Crawford has considered Van der Pol's explanation of reflection in the upper ionosphere where the apparent dielectric constant

$$E = 1 - \frac{4\pi Ne^2}{m w^2} \quad \text{where}$$

$$N = \text{No. of electrons/ c.c}$$
$$m = \text{mass of electron}$$
$$e = \text{charge of electron}$$
$$w = \text{angular frequency of wave}$$

decreases as N decreases and approaches zero for wavelengths of 31.4 meters and N approximately equal to 10^6 electrons/c.c

Under these conditions the electron density is near the critical area where the phase velocity approaches infinity and the group velocity approaches zero.

Appleton objected to this on the grounds that at

such low group velocities, the attenuation of such echoes approached

$$e^{-50} \text{ ie. } \approx 2 \times 10^{-22}$$

Crawford has overcome this objection by the introduction of beam plasma interactions whereby the attenuated reflected wave is first coupled into longitudinal plasma waves traveling parallel to Earth's magnetic field. Should these latter encounter some nonthermal energetic electrons also traveling along the field lines, then the plasma waves could be amplified by selectively removing energy from the electrons. Under these conditions, the group velocities are low (about 1 km/sec.) and the delays, as a consequence, are long.

Furthermore, the limited supply of energetic electrons accounts for rarity and lack of repetition.

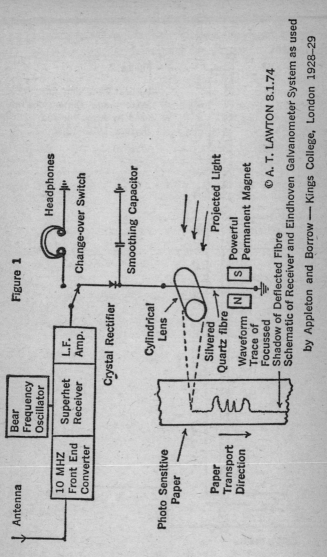

Figure 1

Antenna

| 10 MHZ Front End Converter | Superhet Receiver | Bear Frequency Oscillator |

L.F. Amp.

Headphones

Change-over Switch

Crystal Rectifier

Smoothing Capacitor

Cylindrical Lens

Silvered Quartz fibre

Waveform Trace of Focussed

Shadow of Deflected Fibre

Projected Light

S N Powerful Permanent Magnet

Photo Sensitive Paper

Paper Transport Direction

© A. T. LAWTON 8.1.74
Schematic of Receiver and Eindhoven Galvanometer System as used
by Appleton and Borrow — Kings College, London 1928–29

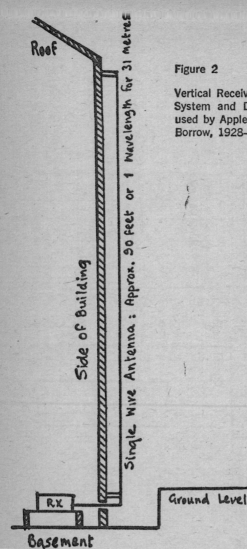

Roof

Side of Building

Single Wire Antenna : Approx. 90 feet or 1 Wavelength for 31 metres

R.X

Basement

Ground Level

Approx. 10 feet

Figure 2

Vertical Receiving Antenna System and Dimensions as used by Appleton and Borrow, 1928–1929.

Figure 3

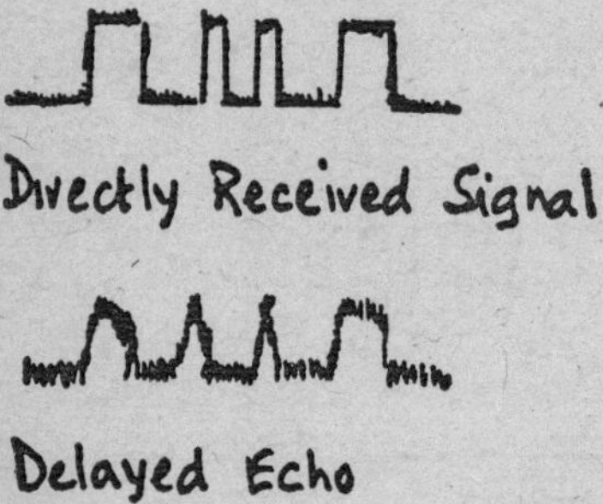

Directly Received Signal

Delayed Echo

Qualitative Characteristics
of the echoes received by
Appleton and Borrow

A.T. LAWTON 1:10:73.

APPENDIX FOUR

RADAR SEARCH OF LAGRANGE AREAS
OF THE MOON

A radar search of the moon libration areas is well within our present capability as shown by the recent experiments in obtaining radar returns from the rings of Saturn. If we assume identical radar parameters are used for Lagrange sounding, then given that:

Saturn is 1320×10^6 km. from Earth

The moon is 400×10^3 km. from Earth,

then the expected Lagrange signal level received would be

$$\left(\frac{1320 \times 10^6}{400 \times 10^3} \right)^4$$

ie. 121×10^{12} greater than that from Saturn.

If we allow the Lagrange reflectance to be only 10^4 of Saturn and further allow a resolution (bandwidth—integrating time) of 10^{-3}, we still have a received signal of 1.21×10^8 greater amplitude.

APPENDIX FIVE

DETAILS OF POSSIBLE SPACE PROBES AND INTERSTELLAR PASSENGER SPACESHIPS

Number of probes launched—500
Weight of each probe at launch—1,000 metric tonnes
Weight of each probe at arrival— <100 metric tonnes
Total weight of probes—500,000 metric tonnes
Number of passenger ships launched—150 (three ships per target planet)
Weight of passenger ship at launch—100,000 metric tonnes
Weight of passenger ship at arrival—80,000 metric tonnes.
Total weight of passenger ships—15 million metric tonnes

Gross tonnage over the entire period of probe and passenger launching (some 500 years) = 15.5 million metric tonnes. This is less than the rate at which our present technology builds ordinary ships in five years.

APPENDIX SIX

ANALYSIS OF DETAIL FROM THE MEMORIAL PLAQUE ON PERSEUS 2

Launching the Ramjets

Gamma Persei is a triple star formed from a pair of "A" type Main Sequence dwarfs rotating around a late G. orange-yellow giant which is off the Main Sequence. The two dwarfs are very close to each other and rotate in a few days. A much greater distance separates this spectroscopic binary "B" component from the giant "A" or major component.

In the topmost section of diagram 10 (Chapter 13) a dotted line starts from the giant star (large circle) and passes between the two dwarfs, curving first around one and then the other. This forms a gravitational "slingshot." The ship is pulled toward one of the dwarf pair, gaining speed as it does so. The ship then passes between the dwarfs. Because of their close proximity, it is likely there will be a hydrogen-rich area as their atmospheres will tend to be drawn together to form a hydrogen cloud or "bridge."

When the ship swings around and approaches this bridge, the magnetic fields of its fusion chamber will be switched on and the hydrogen-helium reaction will start at a high level of thrust. In the rich atmosphere of this bridge, it is likely the motors will develop nearly 50 percent of full thrust when moving at 100 miles/second. This is a speed somewhat lower than that assumed by Bussard (Ref. 1) because the hydrogen particle density in such a bridge is so high.

Indeed it may be necessary to "start up" slowly by passing through the bridge with only a low value of magnetic field. The ship will then swing around and approach the bridge again when the motor may be opened up either to full field and power or sufficiently to allow the ship to move with enough speed to generate the necessary power to accelerate in the weaker density of hydrogen in free space.

The ship may perform several of these "figures of eight" before speeding away from the system. By this time it could be already moving at five to ten percent the speed of light—and still accelerating. A simple chemical rocket such as *Saturn* could almost launch an interstellar probe under such conditions.

The Planetary System

Below the large star circles are five smaller ones representing planets. Alongside these is a humanoid figure in a rectangular frame. The lines at right angles to the frame pick out two of the planets, the first and the third. This means the Perseans lived on the first and moved to the third (as shown by the arrow) which also indicates they had developed space travel. The fact that the movement is shown outward and away from the main star could indicate that this was now an orange-yellow giant off the Main Sequence and growing steadily hotter.

Where the Perseans Went

Below the outline of the spaceship is a tiny Persean figure showing that the race designed a ship with a funnel-shaped intake. Below, the 50 rays or paths radiating outward stop at certain dots representing star constellations. A large arrow points in a direction that a visitor would quickly assume was pointing to an area of the sky around which all other stars revolved—one of the polar regions. At certain times of the year, the constellations depicted would nearly fit some of those seen in the skies.

If a visitor remained long enough, he could also determine how long the plaque had been there, because if Perseus 2 wobbled on its axis, as does Earth, the Pole would have drifted. At present Earth's celestial pole points to Polaris, but 4000 years ago it pointed at Deneb in Cygnus (the Egyptians painted pictures inside the pyramids showing Deneb as the North Star.)

However, it is very likely that the true navigational coordinates of the 50 target stars would have been stored in digital binary form in some permanent record system buried in a sealed cache beneath the beacon antenna. A visitor could translate these 50 sets of coordinates in his spaceship computer.

The Binary Numbers

On the right of the diagram are a series of horizontal and vertical strokes which must be read from left to right—the opposite of normal computer reading. The shortest number has nine "bits" and the largest 32. Applying the simplest code (plain binary) the numbers range from around 512 (2^9) to 4 294 967 296 (2^{32}).

If we take the symbol "-" to be binary "0" and "1" to be binary "1," then, converting to decimals, we have the following:

Decimal: 1 2 4 8 16 32 64 128
Code: 0 1 1 0 1 0 0   1

—that is the sum of 2 + 4 + 16 + 128, ie. 150

Since the number 150 is alongside the spaceship outline it must be assumed that 150 ships were launched. The other binary codes produce the following figures:

Alongside the first planet—8,000 million; the third planet—500 thousand; the small Persean figure—300 thousand. These must, therefore, be population figures.

As there are fifty flight paths to the stars, three ships must have gone to each.

Ref. Bussard R.W. "Galactic Matter and Interstellar Flight," *Astronautica Acta 6,* pages 179–194 (1960).

BIBLIOGRAPHY
AND FURTHER READING

Appleton, E. V. *Nature*, Vol. 122, Dec. 1928.

Ball, J. A. "The Zoo Hypothesis." *Icarus*, Vol. 19, 1973.

Bennet, G. "Medical and Psychological Problems in the 1972 Single-handed Yacht Race." *The Lancet*, Oct. 6, 1973.

Bond, A. "Problems of Interstellar Propulsion." *Spaceflight*, July 1971.

Borrow, R.L.A. Copyrighted notes 1928–29.

Bracewell, R.N. "Communications from Superior Galactic Communities." *Nature*, Vol. 186, 1960.

Bracewell, R.N. "The Opening Message from an Extra-terrestrial Probe" *Astronautics and Aeronautics*, Vol. 11, 1973.

Budden, K.G. "A Search for Radio Echoes of Long Delay." *Jour. Atmos. Terrest. Physics*, Vol. 2, 1952.

Clarke, C.R. "Two Possible Explanations for LDE." *QST.*, Nov. 1971.

Cocconi, G. and Morrison P. "Searching for Interstellar Communications." *Nature*, Vol. 184, Sept. 19, 1959.

Comfort, A. "Effect of Ethoxyquin on the Longevity of C3H Mice." *Nature,* Vol. 299, Jan. 22, 1971.

Crawford, F.W. "Possible Observations and Mechanism of Very Long Delayed Radio Echoes." *Journal of Geophysical Research, Space Physics, V*ol. 75, 1970.

Crick, F. and Orgel, L. "Directed Panspermia." *Icarus,* Vol. 19.

Drake, F.D. *IEE Transactions on Aerospace and Navigational Electronics.* Issues–Sept. 1962, Dec. 1962, March 1963.

Dunphy, J.E. "Surgery in the 21st Century." Read at International Symposium, University of Manchester, England, Sept. 1973.

Edwards, D.F.A. "The Last Frontier." *Spaceflight,* April 1970.

Foster, G.V. "Non-human Artifacts in the Solar System." *Spaceflight,* Dec. 1972.

Galle, J.C. *L 'Onde Electrique,* 1930 p 257–265.

Gooden, B.A. "Hibernation, Hypothermia and Interplanetary Flight." *Spaceflight,* April 1971.

Hapgood, C.H. *Maps of the Ancient Sea Kings.* Chilton Book Co., 1966.

Holmes, D.C. *Search for Life on Other Worlds.* Sterling Pub. Co.

Horsford, C.E.S. "A British Code of Spacelaw." *Spaceflight,* Feb. 1963.

Jackson, A.A., Ryan, M. "Siberian Black Hole." *Nature,* Vol. 245.

Kane, J. "Alpine Glacial Features of Mars." *Nature,* Vol. 244, July 6, 1973.

Kaplan, S.A. *Extraterrestrial Civilisations–2.* English edition, 1971, by Keter Publishers.

Kardashev, N.S., "Transmission of Information by Extraterrestrial Civilisations." *Astronomical Journal,* No. 41, p 282, 1964.

Lawden, D.F. "The Phenomenon of Time Dilation." *Spaceflight,* April 1970.

Lawton, A.T. "The Interpretation of Signals from Space." *Spaceflight,* Vol. 15, 1973.

Lawton, A.T. "Interstellar Communication–Antenna or Artifact?" *Journal B. I. S.,* April 1974.

Lawton, A.T. *Spaceflight,* July 1971. p 241–244.

Lunan, D.A. "Spaceprobe from Epsilon Bootis." *Spaceflight,* Vol. 15, 1973.

Macvey, J.W. "Interstellar Beacons." *Spaceflight,* Jan. 1972.

Maxwell, J.C. *Treatise on Electricity and Magnetism.* Published 1873.

Migot, A. *Tibetian Marches.* Travel Book Club, London.

Mitton, S. *New Scientist,* Aug. 16, 1973. p 380–382.

Molton, P.M. "Evidence for the Existance of Extraterrestrial Life." *Spaceflight,* July 1973.

Oliver, B.M. "Project Cyclops Study Conclusions and Recommendations." *Icarus,* Vol. 19, 1973.

Penrose, R. "Black Holes." *Scientific American,* May 1972.

Powell, C. "Interstellar Flight and Intelligence in the Universe." *Spaceflight,* Dec. 1972.

Pawsey, J.L., Bracewell, R.N. *Radio Astronomy.* Oxford University Press, 1955.

"Project Cyclops" NASA CR 114445, 1972.

Sagan, C. "NASA Project Viking." *Nature,* July 6, 1973.

Sagan, C. "On the Detectivity of Advanced Galactic Civilisations." *Icarus,* Vol. 19, 1973.

Sagan, C., Drake, F.D. "Interstellar Radio Communication and the Frequency Selection Problem." *Nature,* Vol. 245, 1973.

Slesser, M. "Energy Analysis in Policy Making." *New Scientist,* Nov. 1, 1973.

Störmer, C. *Nature,* Vol. 122, Dec. 1928, p 681.

Störmer, C. *Polar Aurorae.* Oxford University Press, 1955.

Strong, J. *Flight to the Stars.* Temple Press.

Strong, J. "Transtellar Navigation." *Spaceflight,* July 1971.

Sullivan, W. *We Are Not Alone.* Hodder & Stoughton, 1965; McGraw-Hill, 1964.

Tesla, Nikola quoted by L.I. Anderson, "Extraterrestrial Radio Transmissions" in letter to *Nature,* Vol 190, April 2, 1961.

Townes and Swartz *Nature,* Vol. 190, April 15, 1960. p 205–208.

Tovmasyan, G.M. *Extraterrestrial Civilisations–1.* English edition published 1967 by Keter Publishers.

Troitsky, V.S., and Kaplan, S.A. Reported work *Tass,* Oct. 16, 1973.

279

Trotsky, V.S., and Kaplan, S.A. Reported work, *Novosti Bulletin,* Oct. 1973.

Van der Pol, B. *Nature,* Vol. 122, Dec. 1928. p 878–879.

Verschuur, G.L. A search for narrow band 21cm wavelength signals from ten nearby stars. *Icarus,* Vol. 19, 1973. p 329–340.

Villard, O.G. Jr., et al. "Long Delayed Echoes—Radios, Flying Saucers' Effect." *QST.,* May 1969.

Villard, O.G. Jr., et al. "There is no Such Thing as a Long-Delayed Echo." *QST.,* Feb. 1970.

Villard, O.G. Jr., et al. "LDE's, Hoaxes, and the Cosmic Repeater Hypothesis." *QST.,* May 1971.

Westing, A.H., Pfeiffer, E.W. "The Cratering of Indochina." *Scientific American,* May 1972.

Ward, B., and Dubos, R. *Only One Earth.* Deutsch, 1972.

INDEX

283